THE WARNING SIGNS:

—Do you avoid eating high-calorie foods like cookies and ice cream in front of people, but gorge on them in private?
—Do you dislike the way your body looks?
—Do you always worry about eating too much?
—Do you lie about how much you eat?
—Do you constantly check yourself out in mirrors to see if you look fat?
—Do you weigh yourself several times a day?
—Do you take laxatives to lose weight?
—Do you take diuretics to lose weight?
—Do you force yourself to vomit to control your weight?

IF YOU ANSWERED YES TO SOME OR ALL OF THESE QUESTIONS, THIS BOOK CAN HELP YOU UNDERSTAND AND OVERCOME YOUR FOOD FEARS.

EATING WITHOUT FEAR

"The stories will strike a familiar chord with anyone who has suffered from bulimia. Victims and their loved ones can derive support and direction from this book."
—JOEL YAGER, M.D.,
director UCLA Adult Outpatient Eating Disorders Clinic, Professor of Psychiatry

EATING
WITHOUT
FEAR

A Guide to Understanding and Overcoming Bulimia

LINDSEY HALL
AND
LEIGH COHN

BANTAM BOOKS
NEW YORK • TORONTO • LONDON • SYDNEY • AUCKLAND

EATING WITHOUT FEAR

A Bantam Book / published by arrangement with Gürze Books

PRINTING HISTORY
*Originally published as BULIMIA: A Guide to Recovery by
Gürze Books
© 1986*

*Sections of this book were previously printed by Gürze Books as
a set of three booklets.*

Updated Bantam edition / February 1990

ISBN 0-553-28377-4

Published simultaneously in the United States and Canada

---

*Bantam Books are published by Bantam Books, a division of
Bantam Doubleday Dell Publishing Group, Inc. Its trademark,
consisting of the words "Bantam Books" and the portrayal of a
rooster, is Registered in U.S. Patent and Trademark Office and in
other countries. Marca Registrada. Bantam Books, 666 Fifth Avenue, New York, New York 10103.*

PRINTED IN THE UNITED STATES OF AMERICA

OPM   0 9 8 7 6 5 4 3 2 1

Contents

PART I
Understanding Bulimia

2 "EAT WITHOUT FEAR"—A TRUE STORY OF THE GORGE-PURGE SYNDROME

PART II

Overcoming Bulimia

3 WHERE TO START

4 GET SUPPORT!

PART III

Resources

Foreword

I am happy to be writing this foreword because Lindsey Hall and I have so much in common. We both suffered from an eating disorder, she from bulimia and I from borderline anorexia nervosa. Like so many eating disorder sufferers, we also had a long history of dieting and poor self-image. Now, we both enjoy a wonderful freedom from diet/weight conflicts and a genuine love for the women that we are. Lastly, we have both shared our experiences in order to help others achieve this freedom and, with it, greater happiness and peace.

You may have been told that once you have bulimia you will always, in some sense, suffer from an eating disorder—that you can learn to "control the symptoms" (i.e., stop bingeing and purging), but that you can never be completely free or "cured." DON'T BELIEVE IT! The good news is that it's not true! Both Lindsey and I never go on diets, effortlessly maintain healthy weights, and eat spontaneously without anxiety or fear. An eating disorder does not make it impossible for you to achieve freedom from diet/weight conflict!—YOU CAN BREAK FREE.

Of course, you have to work at it. Most of us have at some time hoped that one morning we would wake up to discover that our food problems magically vanished during the night. Unfortunately, I've never known this to happen. The truth is that overcoming bulimia takes a lot of what I call "chidish."

What is "chidish"? It stands for Courage, Hard work, Information, Dogged Determination, Insight, Support, and Hope. You will need tremendous Courage, because it is very scary to give up bulimia and forge new ways of coping and living. It will take a lot of Hard work, because the necessary changes require great effort. You will need accurate and helpful Information in order to understand the challenge you face and to find ways of breaking free. It will take Dogged Determination, because recovery is never instant or easy. You will need Insight into yourself and your life so that you can make the changes you need to stop bingeing and purging. And you will definitely need Support from others and continuing Hope that you can indeed break free.

Eating Without Fear will help you with CHIDISH. Lindsey's story of overcoming nine years of bulimia has instilled hope and courage in many who had given up, and her openness will encourage you to reach out for the support you need.

Of course, you have to do all of the hard work and you have to provide the dogged determination. However, the two-week program is an excellent place to start. Lindsey and Leigh have wisely given this program a dual focus: (a) how to stop bingeing and purging, and (b) how to feel better about yourself, cope with problems and negative feelings in new ways, and live a happier life. No program is likely to provide an "instant recovery," but this one provides ideas, insight, and a practical step-by-step way to get started.

Keep in mind that most people who overcome bulimia experience many setbacks and relapses along the way. Don't jump to the conclusion that you are a "failure" if you, too, experience relapses. One of the wonderful things about this book is that even after you have read it cover to cover, you can return to it again and again for reassurance, guidance, and inspiration.

In 1981, I committed myself to freedom from anorexia and diet/weight conflict. I made that goal my number-one priority and promised myself that I would settle for nothing less than success, even if it took the rest of my life—even if I had to be "fat" to be free. As it turned out, neither were necessary. I strongly urge you to focus on your work toward freedom from bulimia as THE MOST IMPORTANT THING IN YOUR LIFE.

You have probably taken this book off the shelf because you or someone you know would like to stop bingeing and purging. That's great! This book will surely speak to your experiences, fears, and hopes. Be sure to realize, however, that overcoming bulimia is not just a matter of finding the "willpower" or the "perfect program." Freedom from bulimia is a matter of finding self-esteem and happiness. What could possibly be more important than that?

I have known the feelings of discouragement, helplessness, guilt, and self-hate which generally accompany an eating disorder. I empathize with you but more importantly I believe in your ability to break free. You can come to love yourself, your body, and your life. Like Lindsey and me, you can be free from bingeing, purging, and all of the painful conflicts with diet and weight. I know that in *Eating Without Fear* you will find a compassionate, self-affirming, self-empowering book to help you toward that end. Good luck and best wishes!

—Susan Kano,
author of *Making Peace With Food*

Introduction

I am wide awake and immediately out of bed. I think back to the night before when I made a new list of what I wanted to get done and how I wanted to be. My husband is not far behind me on his way into the bathroom to get ready for work. Maybe I can sneak onto the scale to see what I weigh this morning before he notices me. I am already in my private world. I feel overjoyed when the scale says that I stayed the same weight as I was the night before, and I can feel that slightly hungry feeling. Maybe IT will stop today, maybe today everything will change. What were the projects I was going to get done?

We eat the same breakfast, except that I take no butter on my toast, no cream in my coffee and never take seconds (until Doug gets out the door). Today I am going to be really good and that means eating certain predetermined portions of food and not taking one more bite than I think I am allowed. I am very careful to see that I don't take more than Doug. I judge by his body. I can feel the tension building. I wish Doug would hurry up and leave so I can get going!

As soon as he shuts the door, I try to get involved with one of the myriad of responsibilities on my list. I hate them all! I just want to crawl into a hole. I don't want to do anything. I'd rather eat. I am alone, I am nervous, I am no good, I always do everything wrong anyway, I am not in control, I can't make it through the day, I know it. It has been the same for so long.

I remember the starchy cereal I ate for breakfast. I am into the bathroom and onto the scale. It measures the same, *BUT I DON'T WANT TO STAY THE SAME!* I want to be thinner! I look in the mirror, I think my thighs are ugly and deformed looking. I see a lumpy, clumsy, pear-shaped wimp. There is always something wrong with what I see. I feel frustrated, trapped in this body, and I don't know what to do about it.

I float to the refrigerator knowing exactly what is there. I begin with last night's brownies. I always begin with the sweets. At first I try to make it look like nothing is missing, but my appetite is huge and I resolve to make another batch of brownies. I know there is half of a bag of cookies in the bathroom, thrown out the night before, and I polish them off immediately. I take some milk so my vomiting will be smoother. I like the full feeling I get after downing a big glass. I get out six pieces of bread and toast one side in the broiler, turn them over and load them with patties of butter and put them under the broiler again till they are bubbling. I take all six pieces on a plate to the television and go back for a bowl of cereal and a banana to have along with them. Before the last toast is finished, I am already preparing the next batch of six more pieces. Maybe another brownie or five, and a couple of large bowlfuls of ice cream, yogurt or cottage cheese. My stomach is stretched into a huge ball below my ribcage. I know I'll have to go into the bathroom soon, but I want to postpone it. I am in never-never land. I am waiting, feeling the pressure,

*pacing the floor in and out of the rooms. Time is
passing. Time is passing. It is getting to be time.*

*I wander aimlessly through each of the rooms again,
tidying, making the whole house neat and put back
together. I finally make the turn into the bathroom. I
brace my feet, pull my hair back and stick my finger
down my throat, stroking twice, and get up a huge pile
of food. Three times, four and another pile of food. I
can see everything come back. I am glad to see those
brownies because they are SO fattening. The rhythm of
the emptying is broken and my head is beginning to
hurt. I stand up feeling dizzy, empty and weak. The
whole episode has taken about an hour.*

For nine years, I binged and vomited up to four and
five times daily. There were very few days without a
binge, and my thoughts of bingeing were always there,
even in my dreams. It was painful and frightening. I do
not binge anymore, but my healing was not an overnight thing. I worked hard and willingly, and underwent an amazing transformation! I have now been free
from bulimia for more than ten years, and am healthy,
happy, in love with my family, and successful as an
artist and businesswoman.

In 1980 when my husband, Leigh Cohn, and I wrote
my story, *Eat Without Fear,* there were no other pub-
lications available on bulimia. The response was tremendous! It inspired and motivated others who were
trying to quit; and, as we learned more about the binge-
purge syndrome, we realized there was much more to
tell our audience.

Over the next few years, we spoke at colleges all
over the country. I was also the first person on national
television to talk about her own bulimia. We have au-

thored a number of booklets as well as a book—
BULIMIA: A Guide to Recovery. Eating Without Fear
is a revised and updated version of that book and is the
result of personal experience, years of involvement
with this subject, and contact with thousands of
bulimics and therapists. The book is divided into three
main parts. The first, "Understanding Bulimia," answers questions often asked about bulimia, and includes my own story, *Eat Without Fear.* The second
section, "Overcoming Bulimia," offers motivation,
support, inspiration, and specific things to do instead
of bingeing. "A Two-Week Program to Stop Bingeing"
is included here. Written in a personal, instructive, inspirational tone, the program includes day-by-day activities, exercises, and written assignments to be used
by bulimics in their recoveries. The instructions are
direct and specific, but they demand attention and
dedication. Anyone interested in bulimia will find valuable information in this section. The third section, a
Resource Section, contains names and addresses of
eating disorders organizations, a reading list, "Specific
Advice for Loved-Ones," and "A Guide for Support
Groups."

Throughout the book are quotes in *italics.* These
were written by the 217 recovered and recovering
bulimics who responded to a questionnaire we mailed
to 1150 individuals who had purchased our booklets.
They were asked to participate in the survey if they had
ever "engaged in bulimia (food binges followed by self-
induced purges, such as vomiting or laxative abuse)."
Two hundred seventeen bulimics responded by our
deadline, answering sixty-two questions and writing
comments on such subjects as: recovering from eating
disorders, therapy options, the role of family and

friends in their cures, and helpful activities in overcoming bulimia. Their honest and personal comments
touched our hearts and offered tremendous insight into
this often secretive food obsession.

The first nine questions requested factual information such as sex, age, the number of years of bulimia,
and length of time actively seeking a cure. The remaining questions asked the bulimics to rank causes,
therapy options, areas of progress, and helpful activities. We also encouraged them to write short essays
on subjects related to overcoming bulimia. The responses were primarily from women (213), most of
them vomited (80%), though many also used other
purges, and just over half had been anorexic as well as
bulimic. The ages ranged from sixteen to fifty-one, with
an average age of twenty-eight. Some had been obsessive about food for as long as twenty-five years, and
others for as short as a few months. The frequency of
binges ranged from twice a week to all day, every day.
Thirty women (14%) considered themselves "cured,"
but another 83% said they were in recovery. One
woman had been trying to stop her bulimia for eighteen
years, another for a few days, 40% had spent between
one and three years "actively" working on a recovery,
and seven said that they were not "seeking a cure."
One common remark was the preference for the words
"recovered" and "recovering" rather than "cured,"
but most women seemed to use them synonymously.
The only apparent element common to all of these
people was that they had an understanding of bulimia
because of their direct experiences with it. They gener-
ously shared their insight with us, and we are passing it
along to you.

Much of this book is addressed to "you," readers

with bulimia; and, since most bulimics are women, we use feminine pronouns. Also, although "I" am the "speaker," Leigh equally contributed to the writing, ideas, and publishing of this effort, and sometimes "we" both speak in the text.

When I first wrote my booklet, *Eat Without Fear,* I did so as a form of purging, a way to finalize my involvement with bulimia. I did not expect or intend to become more involved with this subject. However, sharing my experience has remained an integral part of my life because of the effect it has had on others. In addition to writing and speaking about overcoming bulimia, recovery issues, and raising self-esteem, Leigh and I also reach out by editing and distributing a catalogue of books which is used as a resource by thousands of people concerned with eating disorders. (See the "Reading List" in Part III.)

My recovery started as a way of loving myself; I hope some of that love reaches you.

Understanding Bulimia

1

Questions Most Often Asked About Bulimia

What is bulimia?

Bulimia is a food obsession characterized by repeated overeating binges followed by purges of forced vomiting, prolonged fasting, excessive exercise, sleeping, or abuse of laxatives, enemas, or diuretics. For an epidemic number of women and men, bulimia is a secret addiction that dominates their thoughts, severely undercuts their self-esteem, and actually threatens their lives. The symptoms are described by the Egyptians, and in the Hebrew Talmud; and, bulimia (Greek for "ox-hunger") was widely practiced during Greek and Roman times. It has also been called bulimia nervosa and bulimarexia.

In 1980, the American Psychiatric Association formally recognized bulimia in its third edition of *Diagnostic and Statistical Manual of Mental Disorders.* The criteria was revised in 1987:

A. Recurrent episodes of binge eating (rapid consumption of a large amount in a discrete period of time, usually less than two hours).

B. A feeling of lack of control over eating behavior during the eating binges.

C. The person regularly engages in either self-induced vomiting, strict dieting or fasting, or vigorous exercise in order to prevent weight gain.

D. A minimum average of two binge eating episodes a week for at least three months.

E. Persistent overconcern with body shape and weight.

(The American Psychiatric Association, Washington, D.C., 1980, 1987).

Most bulimics are women, but it is difficult to say how many people have bulimia. Statistics may not truly reflect the total numbers because bulimics are generally secretive about their behavior. In fact, college students have answered questionnaires more truthfully when told to put a dab of their saliva on the survey paper, because they believed it could be chemically analyzed to determine if they were bulimic! Of the hundreds of studies done on the prevalence of eating disorders, the most reliable statistics indicate that about 8% of women and 1% of men meet the clinical criteria for bulimia (*The Etiology of Bulimia Nervosa*, Craig Johnson & Mary E. Connors; Basic Books, New York, c. 1987). However, some studies report much higher numbers. Whatever the actual figures, there are a tremendous number of bulimic women and a high number of men.

Is it dangerous?

Absolutely! Excessive vomiting can cause death from cardiac arrest, kidney failure, impaired metabolism due to electrolyte imbalance, or severe dehydration. Other serious physical side-effects include rotten teeth, digestive disorders, amenorrhea, malnourishment, anemia, infected glands, blisters in the throat, internal bleeding, hypoglycemia, icy hands and feet, and a ruptured stomach or esophagus.

Laxative abuse can irritate intestinal nerve endings, which can inhibit them from triggering contractions. Heavy use of laxatives or enemas removes protective mucus from the intestinal lining, which can result in bowel infections. The lower bowel can lose muscle tone, becoming limp and unable to produce contractions. Dehydration and fluid imbalances can occur with the same side-effects as listed above. Also, laxative abusers often have rectal pain, gas, constipation, diarrhea (or both), and bowel tumors.

There are emotional side-effects to bulimia as well, including social isolation, fear, generalized anxiety, loneliness, and low self-esteem. These emotions are blanketed by obsessive thoughts about food, secret rituals, and gorge-purge behavior. The binges associated with bulimia provide an instant numbness which is highly addictive.

Why do people become bulimic?

There is no easy answer. Bulimia is generally considered to be a psychological and emotional disorder, but there are significant studies that claim bulimia is related to major affective disorder, and might be caused by heredity and chemical imbalances in the body. (See our answer to "Can I take a drug to get better?") The reasons most people give for their bulimia are childhood conflicts and cultural pressures. Many started because purging seemed like a good way to diet, but once their bingeing and purging cycle began, the resulting metabolic imbalances and habitual escape became an addiction.

People become addicted to avoid painful feelings—past as well as present. Some of these feelings have their origins in childhood, such as feeling unloved and unlovable, ashamed and afraid, and even cut off from themselves. Some of these feelings may come from the pressure to conform, to be accepted by peers, or from the competition generated by our cultural ideals of success and beauty. Most devastating of all are the feelings associated with low self-esteem: that we have no worth, that our lives have no value or purpose, and that we will never be fullfilled or happy.

Still, the question remains as to why bulimia is the chosen escape. There appear to be similarities in the backgrounds and personalities of eating disordered individuals which will help clarify this. All of these will not apply to every case, but certainly some will.

Most bulimics come from dysfunctional families in which the emotional, physical, and spiritual needs of family members are not met. In many of these households, feelings are not verbally expressed. There is often a history of depression, alcoholism, drug abuse, or eating disorders, and the child might unconsciously recognize these as acceptable avenues for escape. Additionally, recent studies suggest that more than half of all bulimic women were victims of incest or sexual abuse.

Bulimics are often considered "ideal" children, and will go out of their way to be "people pleasers." (Food is a "good girl's" drug.) They present an acceptable facade—seeming outgoing, confident, and independent—while anxious feelings bubble underneath. They may be loved for not needing to be nurtured, for taking care of themselves, and for growing up early. Out of an unfullfilled need for recognition, they may develop insecurities about their appearance, competence, and ability to be loved. Personality traits often exist in conflict, such as: a craving for nurturance and a fear of intimacy, an ability to "mother" plants, animals and other people but not themselves, and the desire to be in control and to lose it. Bulimics also tend to be judgmental of themselves and others, have difficulty expressing emotions through language, fear criticism, avoid disagreements, and have extremely low self-esteem.

Sometimes, people become bulimic to postpone growing up. The child who has looked to others for validation and feelings of self-worth and who has assumed a "perfect little girl" role because it works at home may experience tremendous fear at having to trust herself and face the outside world alone. This insecurity is sometimes unconsciously reinforced by parents who also do not want to let go.

The bulimics from our survey identified various causes for their bulimia. Many remembered specific reasons for their initial binges, as well as how the behavior subsequently served them. Few women thought it would become addictive. In addition to the original causes, which still existed, they were faced with guilt, secrecy, physical side-effects, and an increasing number of reasons to use bulimia. They were asked to rate the influence of several causes, and their totals ranked in this order: the influences of media and culture, family dynamics, mental "numbness," and the taste of food. Also frequently mentioned were: boredom, a failed diet, death of a loved one, sexual tension, and organic problems.

This recovered bulimic understands that despite the causes for her bulimia, she had the power to overcome those causes:

It was extremely important for me to realize that I **chose** *this as a coping mechanism. Yes, outside circumstances were what they were, but they did not cause my compulsive behavior.*

Most bulimics have been preoccupied with eating and diet for years, but the initial binge-purge episodes might be triggered by specific events, such as: traumatic change (graduation, moving away from home, marriage, etc.), unresolved grief (I was deeply affected by the death of a pet), career changes, a failed diet, and rejection by a lover or wished-for lover. These survey comments were among the several specific reasons offered for starting the bulimic behavior.

I have lots of menstrual problems and hormonal imbalances. My food pattern is definitely related to this. Before my period, I hit such a "low" that I feel like giving up. Trying to keep away from bingeing is so much harder during this time.

I started because I was rejected by a boy at age fifteen. Since I liked myself, I really felt the only thing wrong with me was my weight.

I first developed my eating disorder the night before my first college finals. My father had passed away a month earlier, and I was nervous about finals and about returning home and having him not be there.

I had been dieting for a couple of weeks, and was getting tired of it.

I never thought about trying it until I read about it.

I started throwing up binges during my fourth month of pregnancy, when I could not handle my changing body and dieting away the calories became impossible.

No matter what the underlying reasons for choosing bulimia as a method of coping with painful feelings are, the fact is that bulimia works on many different levels—binge-eating provides instant relief. The mind ceases to dwell on anything but food and how to get it down. It replaces all other actions, thoughts, and emotions. Even vomiting can be pleasurable when it is the most intimate contact we allow with our own bodies. When the whole binge/purge episode is over, for a brief moment, the bulimic regains control. No longer feeling guilty for having eaten so many calories the bulimic is drained, relaxed, and high.

Since bulimia does not seem to be dangerous compared to other addictions such as alcoholism or drug abuse, it is especially insidious and captivating. (See our answer to "Is it dangerous?") Food is always available for a "fix," and eating in public, even if on the run, is accepted and not unusual. There is also nothing to give a bulimic away because her body weight appears close to normal. Food gives life, it heals, nurtures, and means love. The safety, relief, availability, pleasure, and companionship represented by food far outweigh any immediate drawbacks. It is a short-term solution for life-long stress.

Why are bulimics mainly women?

The fact is that epidemic numbers of women are overeating and vomiting on a regular basis. There are countless more with other types of eating disorders and a preoccupation with thinness and dieting. Considerably fewer bulimics are men, and there is little data available on this population. Some male athletes who purged to "make weight," such as wrestlers and jockeys, subsequently developed bulimia. Overall, male bulimics seem to have many of the same clinical characteristics as the female bulimic population but are significantly fewer in number. While there are theories that women are predisposed to bulimia for biological reasons, perhaps pertaining to the hypothalamus, we must examine our culture and common backgrounds to understand how women in particular are affected.

While it is true that men and women are naturally concerned with attraction, along the path through puberty, adolesence, and adulthood, women get the message that how they look is more important than what they think, do, or feel. When sexual game-playing starts, one of the most pernicious lessons is that girls should look pretty for boys. What's more, girls learn to expect rewards for what are stereotypically termed "feminine" traits, such as: docility, unselfishness, politeness, and sometimes being a tease. The implied rewards are not insignificant either. Great bodies are falsely equated with great sex and happiness, marriage, feelings of self-worth, will-power, independence, fulfillment, success, and an overall glamorous life.

Furthermore, the ideal body is presented not only as desirable but also as attainable, if only women can get CONTROL. It is believed that anyone can get thinner if they try hard enough, and most women keep trying!

Even some with model-thin figures think there are pounds to be lost and happiness to be gained, thereby. Women become bulimic because there appears to be no end to this struggle. It's an ideal release. Step out from under pressure, furiously eat for an hour, then turn back the clock by vomiting it all up.

One momentous influence on my generation was the electronic babysitter, television. In the shows that we watched, the couples were usually happily married, the husband responsible for the income and emotional strength, and the women responsible for homemaking, childrearing, and being attractive, loving wives. In fact, many women who later became bulimic saw their parents and other adults in those same roles. There were no other apparent options. Today, television's impact on women is stronger than ever. While there are an increasing number of strong female characters, most are still the happy housewives, confused career women, sexy detectives, unable to be assertive in honest relationships, and just as pretty as could be! What's more, actresses and thin models are used to sell everything imaginable; and, it's not surprising that many of these women, who are paid enormous sums for their "look" and skinny bodies, are themselves bulimic. The make-believe world of television played no small part in establishing in the minds of many a fantasy that they could be happy, loved, and desired if only they looked thin and beautiful.

This myth is perpetuated by a media blitz which encourages women to look like emaciated models, buy into innumerable diet plans, and eat every kind of food sold. The conflict between eating and staying thin comes up in virtually every popular magazine. One "ladies" magazine printed an excellent article on bulimia, which was interrupted by a two-page advertisement for a cake mix! Women are supposed to bake the cakes, but not eat them. Bulimics, however, can eat as much as they want and gain no weight by purging themselves! These same media sell women fashions that promote the concept of women as sexual objects—delicious, flawless, aloof. No wonder there are so many bulimics squeezed into uncomfortable jeans and identities, avoiding intimate relationships for the solitary numbness of bingeing.

Women are also traditionally limited by cultural stereotypes in the marketplace and in the political arena. The majority of working women are in low-paying clerical and service-oriented jobs. Those who land rewarding jobs in the areas of their interest and expertise are often under tremendous pressure. In either case, bulimia can be one way of letting off steam.

The conflict between eating and the fear of getting fat was a central issue in survey comments. Many addressed society's standards of beauty, economics of advertising, and how media bombards consumers with skinny women, unrealistic relationships, and sugary, fast foods. While a cover girl's photo or ice cream advertisement did not cause a binge, these reminders that thinner equals better established values that led to distorted ways of viewing food and the self. More than one-third of the surveys identified media and culture as major causes. This bulimic of twelve years, who has recovered, needed to re-evaluate her thinking:

I had to change my value system. Once only pursuing thinness, I had to question its real value. I had to get angry at fashion models and TV commercials. I felt sorry for individuals whose main focus in life was how skinny they could get, because it meant that they were basically and intensely unhappy. I had to question who

I was trying to be skinny for, and why I was so con-cerned by what others thought of me. I had to re-learn what I wanted for me. It came down to learning about my likes and dislikes. I had to learn what I was in-tensely interested in—something that took my mind off of the attitudes and behaviors of my disorder.

These women identified cultural pressures to being thin:

Fear of gaining weight caused me to start purging when I binged. Supposedly "thin is in" and you won't be accepted if you're fat.

The whole "thinness" culture was a big influence.

*I became starved for human relationships. Bulimia works. By remaining attractively thin, I can draw peo-ple to me. By appearing perfect, I can keep them from getting **too close**. My therapy is aimed at learning to be honest and to trust enough to be vulnerable.*

Is it the same as anorexia nervosa?

For many years bulimia was considered to be one type of anorexic behavior. By recognizing bulimia as a separate disorder in **DSM-III,** the American Psychi-atric Association isolated a much larger group than those who could be clinically classified as anorexic. Although many of the issues surrounding these eating disorders are related, and many anorexics also purge, anorexia nervosa is characterized by self-starvation; and, the clinical diagnosis includes the loss of 25% of body weight. In both cases, the relationship with food is a symptom of other serious problems. However, in general, anorexics reject food, have lower body weight, are younger, and are socially and sexually less mature. In contrast, the majority of bulimics' weight appear closer to normal, most began purging in their late teens or early twenties (many anorexics turn to bulimia), and are more socially outgoing. Hospitalization is often necessary for anorexics, who have a high fatality rate—10–15% of anorexics die from the disease. There is no current data for bulimia fatality statistics, but the clinical impression is that they are low, and definitely not as high as for anorexia nervosa.

Eating and vomiting was easier for me than starving, so I was never anorexic. I sometimes wished for the power to starve, but I never could!

What is a typical binge?

"Typical" depends entirely on the individual. The size and frequency can vary as well as the type of purge and the length of time between sessions. However, many bulimics have said that they can "relate to" my binges, which I describe in the chapter, "Eat Without Fear." During one of my typical binges, I probably took in 5000 calories before throwing up. Compare that to the 1800 to 2300 calories that a healthy young woman between 5'3" and 5'10" normally consumes. Over the course of a day with several binges, my intake may have reached 30,000 to 40,000 calories—three weeks' worth of food!

Frequently I started a binge while in the course of eating what I thought to be a "good" or "safe" meal. For example, I may have gone to a salad bar and carefully allowed myself a moderate portion. As I ate the salad, I began to feel guilty about sugar that was in the salad dressing. Then it started to bother me that I had taken croutons. At one point in the meal, I decided I had eaten one bite too many. Rather than stop eating, I'd think, "What's the difference, I might as well finish my salad because it tastes so good. I've already gone too far. I'll do a binge, and none of the calories will matter after I vomit."

If I had my choice, I would eat sweets and refined carbohydrates. A single binge might include: a quart of ice cream, a bag of cookies, a couple of batches of brownies, a dozen donuts, and a few candy bars. When I was desperate, I would binge on anything: oatmeal, cottage cheese, carrots, or day-old rolls that I fished out of the trash from what was to be my last-ever binge.

My stomach stretched so much that I looked pregnant, and I usually postponed vomiting for about 30 minutes of numbness. Then I'd stick my fingers down my throat until I had vomited everything that would come up. The whole episode lasted about an hour, and I often felt very weak and dizzy afterwards. Personally, I never abused laxatives, enemas, or diuretics.

What does it feel like to binge-vomit?

The mental "numbness" and physical "high" are important reasons that the binge-vomiting becomes so addictive. In fact, many women from our survey who were compulsive about food were also alcoholics, or came from families where substance abuse existed. Bingeing temporarily removes stress, like a drug. In my case, after purging, I expected that everything would be better; and, that I would never binge again. Once my "high" had ended, I usually started another binge. For more than five years, I binged and vomited four or five times—and more—practically every day. I also sometimes had sexual feelings from the emerging, private excitement, complete involvement, fullness, stroking, and sudden release. This added to the "high." Several surveyed women commented about the drug-like aspect of bulimia:

I can easily see how during stressful times of your life you seek some kind of comfort. I found this in food, others find it in drugs and alcohol. All are bad habits that are so hard to break. They are harmful mentally and physically.

I like the high and then the numbness.

When I first tried to give up my bulimic behaviors, I began to drink more alcohol. I was substituting one escape for another. I would get so depressed over my drinking that I would finally binge. I have now joined Alcoholics Anonymous, have been sober five months, and find my bulimia much more manageable. I am now recovered, but until I quit drinking I kept having recurrent episodes of my old bulimic behavior.

I don't binge when I start drinking alcohol. I am afraid if I keep this up, I might become an alcoholic.

Before I started therapy, I never associated my desire to binge with my emotions. I always felt it was an uncontrollable desire for huge amounts of food. Now I understand the binge takes the place of allowing myself to feel any emotions.

No matter how down and depressed you feel, think of food as a temporary filling or "high." Find something permanent, because after you purge, you'll feel the same or even worse. Why waste your time?

Do bulimics share other behaviors besides overeating and vomiting?

People with eating disorders have compulsive personalities; the rituals they create are safe and familiar places to reside. Many of their rituals revolve around food and body image, such as arranging food on their plates, excessive exercise, eating systematically, and obsessive calorie counting. Some behaviors are not related to food, such as: always knowing where the nearest bathroom is, lying, keeping secrets, and kleptomania.

Most bulimics take exhaustive steps to cover up their bingeing. During the five years of my first marriage, my husband never found out about my closely guarded secrets. No one knew! Covering my tracks was part of my daily routine. Lying about food was second nature to me. For example, if I went to the same grocery daily to buy large quantities of binge food, I would tell the checkers that I was a nursery school teacher buying snacks for the children. My rituals included a preoccupation with scales, mirrors, and trying on clothes. I used to weigh myself before and after binges to be sure that I gained no weight. At one point in my recovery, I took a hammer to the scale! I also used to try on all my clothes, checking myself in a full-length mirror to be sure that the clothes still fit and I was not getting any fatter. Actually, I could not pass any mirror without fully checking myself out.

There is also an exceptionally high incidence of kleptomania among bulimics. In our survey, 37% of the bulimics mentioned kleptomania. Eating binges can get quite expensive, and one way to offset the cost of food is to steal it! I shoplifted food, but stopped when I got caught with a container of artificial sweetener.

However, there is usually more to kleptomania than just basic economics. In my case, I wanted the love, attention, and approval of my parents; and, not being able to get those emotional rewards, I sought to take temporarily satisfying items such as clothing or jewelry. I also felt unworthy and incapable of affording "nice" things, although I spent vast amounts on food. Since curing myself of bulimia, I am confident that I can fill my needs myself, and I no longer have any desire to steal. The women in our survey had similar experiences. Their stealing ranged from candy bars to larger, more expensive items. Most of those who stole also indicated that it was not too difficult a pattern to change. A few women were arrested, and stopped immediately, such as this one:

I stopped stealing after I got caught with a chicken in my purse!

How do I know if I have it?

Have we been talking about you? I binged and vomited daily for nine years without knowing that I had a "disease." When I read a magazine article about bulimia, I became aware for the first time that there were other people who had the same eating behavior as mine.

Bulimics can become addicted to the gorge-purge syndrome on a daily basis or can continue with occasional binges for many years. Whether you binge and force yourself to vomit daily or only on weekends, you are still abusing your body. Even if you are obsessive only in your thoughts about weight, diet, and food, you have a food problem, although maybe not the clinical definition of bulimia. I know of no one who does not

njoy an occasional large meal (holiday binges!), but an
bsession is an escape. If you have food obsessions,
ou have a problem, regardless of the "title."

How long will it last?

That's up to you. It is obvious that the behavior does
ot suddenly stop without an effort. Although bulimia
nay start as a diet, its addictive nature can continue as
life-long obsession. I have corresponded with a
voman in her sixties who has been bulimic for more
han forty years. In the past, so little was known about
ulimia that women commonly continued for years
efore seeking an end to their bingeing. When I was
ulimic, there was practically nothing written or pub-
cized about the syndrome, but now bulimics are more
ware that their habits are dangerous, so cures are
ought earlier.

How long does it take to get better?

There are a few steps to getting over bulimia. The
rst is making the decision to seek a cure. From that
me till the bingeing is completely stopped varies. I
ave heard of people who have gone "cold turkey,"
nd stopped instantly, but most people take longer. It
ook me about one year.

However, ridding myself of the obsessive thoughts
bout my body has taken longer. I worked hard not to
e affected by cultural stereotypes, and I learned to
ove my own unique shape. There was a time when
nly one binge each month seemed like an impossible
oal. Now, I hardly ever think about it, and I have not
inged for several years. During menstruation, I crave

and eat more food than usual, especially sweets. Thi
reminds me of my bulimia, that's all.

Just as no one forces a bulimic to binge, no one ca
force them to stop. For some people, prolonge
therapy, or even hospitalization, is necessary. Gener
ally, overcoming bulimia takes time and a firm commit
ment, and increased effort and determination wi
make it happen faster.

Will I always be bulimic?

Some people may try to convince you that you wi
be, but I am not one of them. I was bulimic for nin
years, spent a year and a half quitting the behavior, an
gradually have let go of the beliefs, values, and ways c
relating to others which supported and even encour
aged my bulimia. I can now honestly say that *I am n
longer bulimic*.

It may be necessary to depend on another behavio
such as exercise or shopping, to relieve tension o
distract yourself, and there is the possibility that yo
will just trade one compulsivity for another. Howeve
if you continually ask yourself if the steps you ar
taking are in a more positive direction, gradually yo
will be able to let go of all compulsivity. There wi
come a time when days pass without any fears assoc
ated with what you eat or look like. Remember, you ar
a worthwhile and important soul whose compulsivitie
are serving you in many ways. Be patient, be gentle
and let them go.

How will I know I'm cured?

Again, part of being "cured" is creating your ow
definitions. Look to yourself for the answer to this on

because only you will know when your thoughts are not constantly directed towards food. As I have said, it is a gradual process, and only you can know if it's over. I used the word "cured" when I stopped the binge-purge behavior but I've also been getting more "cured" with time. I now consider myself 100% free of eating disorders, and I fully believe that this is possible for others, as well.

Can I take a drug to get better?

It might help, but even the strongest proponents of drug therapy do not recommend treatment based entirely on pills. Still, recent scientific data does support the use of MAO-inhibitors and tricyclic antidepressants for the treatment of select patients with bulimia.

This is a very controversial subject among clinicians. Most agree that individuals with eating disorders have mood disturbances, and many argue that bulimia is related to major affective disorder—the psychiatric family under which major depression is classified. There is also evidence suggesting that the cause of eating disorders might be traced to hereditary, genetic, and biological factors, including abnormalities of the hypothalamus, a gland in the brain which regulates many bodily functions.

A high percentage of bulimics have responded well to drug treatment and have lost the cravings to binge within weeks; but antidepressants do not work for everyone, nor will any kind of treatment. Draw your own conclusions by consulting with a psychiatrist trained in the pharamacological treatment of bulimia.

Two books which discuss this issue are *The Role of Drug Treatments for Eating Disorders* and *New Hope for Binge Eaters*. (See Reading List.)

We do not have direct experience with drug treatment; therefore, we cannot recommend or criticize this approach. Let us make these observations: Any form of help that works for you is worthwhile. If taking a pill will stop you from bingeing and give you an experience of wellness to motivate you, fine. After all, if you have a headache you'd probably take an aspirin. This does not mean that you should stop reading our book or using the techniques that we promote! Stopping your bingeing is only part of your goal. Whether you choose to investigate drug therapy or not, you still must face the issues in your life that propel you towards the binge-purge behavior.

How do I learn to eat correctly?

Once you stop obsessing, you can decide what and how much you want to eat. A qualified dietitian or nutritionist can provide a specific program, and it is helpful to watch other people eat. We recommend eating moderate portions instead of bingeing, and not feeling guilty. Bulimics have certain foods which trigger fears about weight gain, typically: chocolate, butter, cream, breads, etc. Rather than completely eliminating these foods, enjoy them in limited quantities. This takes permission, which may be something you need to practice. During my cure, I insisted upon having a daily sweet, if only a taste of someone else's dessert. Eventually, I was able to eat my own without feeling guilty. I also found that tasting new and different foods helped me to feel satisfied by what I ate. (This topic is addressed further in the "Getting Past Food Fears" chapter.)

If I quit vomiting, will I gain weight?

There is no one answer to this question that is true for everyone. Some people do gain weight, others lose or stay the same. According to the results of our survey, of the bulimics who were trying to end their bulimia, 41% answered that they gained, usually 5–10 pounds. There were some who lost weight, also usually 5–10 pounds, but nearly half recorded either no change or that their weight fluctuated up and down. This question brings up two other questions: Why do you want to lose weight, and can you lose weight in a healthy manner?

Let's acknowledge some issues regarding dieting and weight loss. DIETING DOES NOT WORK. At any given moment, some 20 million Americans are actively dieting, and 98% of them will fail to lose weight and keep it off. In our society today, there are implied rewards to thinness, but this has not always been the case. For the past twenty years, analysts have also shown that centerfolds and beauty contestants have gotten continually thinner. Ironically, many of today's models and starlets, while pitching diet sodas and cosmetics, are the same women who are also unhappily fighting with eating disorders to stay thin and marketable. Who decides whether it's okay to be heavy or thin, and why? Every popular medium is overloaded with diet plans, and new diet books hit the bookshelves practically every day. Face it, the diet craze has led to wealth for many people, and they all want to keep selling. Besides diet plans, foods and drinks, health spas, weight-loss centers, aerobics videos, and exercise equipment, consider the clothing industry. Not only do they sell garments designed to highlight your slim figure, they actually make greater profits by using less fabric on smaller sizes! If all this doesn't make you feel angry and manipulated, it should! Obsessing about weight instead of confronting personal and global issues is just another way of remaining isolated, ineffective, and unhappy. Being thinner will not help you to find lasting love, it won't improve your "lot" in life, and it won't bring peace to the world. Basically, obsessive dieting will only help others get rich and bring you trouble.

One reason often given to explain why a diet might not work is explained by the theory of "setpoint." According to this theory, everyone has a genetically determined weight which is best for them—physically and emotionally. For some people this weight might be high, for others low. This can be hard to accept, especially if we have always looked for our ideal weights on standardized tables and skinny models instead of within our own bodies. The fact is, though, that we can usually find our dress sizes on our family trees, and there is not much we can do about it!

The setpoint operates like an appetite and metabolic thermostat. If we undereat, the metabolism slows down and burns fewer calories while our hunger increases. If we overeat, the metabolism speeds up, burns more calories, and our appetite drops. In this way, the body actually defends a particular weight in an effort to maintain health and balance. So long as we are not starving or stuffing ourselves, we can eat a variety of foods—more on some days and less on others—and keep a relatively stable weight.

Actually, there is not one ideal weight for each of us, but an ideal weight range, which is about five to ten percent of total body weight. We can lower our setpoint somewhat, therefore, by increasing the amount of healthy aerobic exercise we get, choosing whole grains rather than refined carbohydrates, and decreasing fats and simple sugars. But dieting, purging, or any other method of trying to attain a weight that is significantly lower than this setpoint range will create physical hunger, tension, depression, anger, feelings of deprivation, and a preoccupation with food. In other words, your body is telling you it needs more nourishment.

This is why it is important to ask yourself why you really want to be thin. What will you gain that is worth this denial and emotional distress? Dieting is an endless struggle, because what you think you "should" weigh and what your body wants to weigh are two different numbers.

For this reason, frightening though it may be, many bulimics who resume normal eating do gain weight. At the same time, though, they are making the commitment to gain happiness, peace of mind, feelings of wholeness and integrity, as well as taking care of themselves emotionally and physically. The quotes from our survey illustrate the common realization many women had—that weight and appearance were not as important as they once seemed. This thirty-four-year-old bulimic was a compulsive binger for five years before entering professional therapy. Her case demonstrates a radical example:

My weight increased by thirty pounds, then I fasted fifty-five pounds off, have since regained it all, and am finally learning to accept myself. As a result, I've begun to slowly lose some weight, but it isn't nearly as important as it used to be. My cure is almost complete.

These quotes reflect more typical experiences:

My weight stays within a five-pound range. I will admit that I would like to weigh about five pounds less, but I consider stopping bulimia much more important than being "thin."

This increase (eight pounds) was right after I stopped vomiting every day, but I have stayed at that weight ever since.

I'm content with myself and realize I don't have to be skinny any longer. My health is more important to me than the image of "model thin."

How should I choose a therapist?

Most bulimics who want to cure themselves should consider professional therapy. I'm often asked for referrals for therapists, and I used to offer names, thinking that anyone familiar with bulimia would be helpful to someone looking for a therapist. At one lecture, I recommended a psychiatrist who was considered a national expert on eating disorders. From the back of the room, a woman immediately cried out, "Oh no, that man is horrible." She went on to describe her experiences with him, which were indeed terrible. Yet I know that he has helped others. It is important to find the therapist that is right for you. Would you buy a car without a test drive? I've seen people literally spend an hour trying to decide which ice cream to pick in a supermarket. Choosing a therapist should certainly take more consideration than that. Put in time and effort to find a therapist that will help you.

Finding and selecting a therapist requires work. Local health agencies usually provide lists of doctors and counselors who treat bulimia, and hospitals and medical clinics often have specialists in this area. A "therapist" is usually a psychiatrist, psychologist, or marriage and family counselor; but, there are other professionals who can also help, such as: licensed social workers, nutritionists, clergymen, acupuncturists, or chiropractors. Check in the phone book and make some calls asking for references. Referrals are a good place to start, but you have to kick their tires! Most professionals will allow you to interview them. Call their office and ask for a short no-charge appointment to meet them. This is their profession and they want you to trust and respect them. Let them know that you are also interviewing other therapists—they'll appreciate your effort.

Another important consideration is whether you are interested in trying antidepressants. Only qualified physicians can prescribe drugs. You will want to find a psychiatrist who is familiar with both the use of antidepressants and the treatment of bulimia.

Come prepared with a list of questions. This will not be a therapy session, so your questions can be hypothetical or direct—it's up to you. Some things you might ask are: What is their approach to bulimia? How often would you need to see them? How quickly might you see results? How long would they expect therapy to last? What will the charges be and do they have a sliding fee, based upon income and need? Do they accept your insurance?

In evaluating the interviews, use criteria that are meaningful to you. These are subjective measures. Probably the most important area to consider is how you felt during the interviews. If you were comfortable with the therapist and felt that you could honestly work with him or her, that's a good indication. If they impress you with their knowledge and expertise, can you relate to them? Other things to notice: Do you like the office? Does the staff seem friendly? Does the therapist answer you directly or invite you to express yourself?

Finally, you can always change therapists. Once you've picked out someone, try a few sessions. Give therapy a chance. You might decide together on a reasonable time period before evaluating your progress. If therapy with your first choice proves unsatisfactory, find someone else!

(Be sure to read the "Professsional Therapy" section in the "Where to Start" chapter of this book.)

Will I have to be hospitalized?

Everyone's recovery process is different. For some bulimics, hospitalization is an effective part of their treatment. Rarely would it be a first option unless there were serious medical complications resulting from bingeing and purging. There are many hospital programs that specialize in eating disorders and specifically bulimia. Whether or not one of these programs would be appropriate for you is something that you should discuss with your therapist or doctor.

I care about someone who is bulimic, what can I do to help?

You can tell them that you care about them and offer your support. Let them know that you don't despise them for their eating problems, or think that they are disgusting. If they can open up to you with their emotions and honest feelings, it will surely help. Encourage and love them, but remember that they are the ones with the problem. Do not expect them to suddenly change unless they can come to this realization themselves. Suggest support groups or give them copies of books you have found helpful in your own search for peace.

Parents of bulimics need to be aware of limitations in helping their children. In many instances, parents have played a major role in the cause of the child's behavior, and they may have to undergo some changes of their own. They may need to examine their own values and ways of communicating and then try to understand their child's problem. Guilt, anger, frustration, denial, and cynicism are all likely sentiments. They might be accompanied by a desperate determination to make the child change. With patience, love, and increased self-knowledge, parents can better accept their own feelings and begin to help their child. (Anyone wanting to help someone with bulimia should be sure to read our chapter, "Specific Advice for Loved Ones.")

C H A P T E R

2

"Eat Without Fear"—A True Story of the Gorge-Purge Syndrome

Introduction

I finished writing *Eat Without Fear* on my birthday in 1980. I printed 100 copies of my 32-page booklet, and finally felt completely free from bulimia. Telling my story so fully was an ultimate purge for me! At that time there were no books solely about bulimia, so it was important to let people know about this secretive obsession.

Since that time, I have been involved with bulimia as a writer and educator. Along with my husband, Leigh Cohn, who co-wrote *Eat Without Fear,* we have brought bulimia to the attention of many thousands of readers. About 40,000 copies of my story have been read, and the response to it and our other booklets, books, tapes, and lectures has been tremendous. We've loved the many letters from readers who have been inspired and motivated in their recoveries.

Beginning

I came from an affluent family that lived in a fancy home an hour north of New York City. My father commuted to the city where he worked as an investment banker. My mother was active in environmental causes, country club tennis, and amateur photography. I had three older siblings who paid little attention to me—except for one sister who teased me unmercifully. I was seven when the fifth child was born, and my parents hired a live-in couple to take care of me and my baby brother.

The overall impression I have of my childhood is of being alone and afraid that I had done something wrong. I didn't mean to get in trouble; on the contrary, I always tried to be a perfect little girl. Nevertheless, I had the perception that I was constantly screwing up, like the time I hid my brother's watch in cornstarch when he was chasing me, unaware of the damage that would be caused; or when I put my sister's toy animals in a pillowcase to show to someone, not realizing they were delicate china and would all break. My father made me suffer for that mistake! One of my biggest goof-ups was getting locked in my mother's clothes closet where I had gone to test a tie with a light on it. She went to New York, and I stayed locked away all day, crying and afraid. No one heard my screams, not the maid, the laundress, or my nanny. I was not found until my mother came home late that afternoon. Even though I was rescued, I felt like life in that house could go on without me and no one would notice. I was not the smartest, prettiest, oldest, youngest, or a boy, any of which, I thought, would have given me some importance in the household.

Most of the time, I retreated alone to my room, attic playroom, or the barns to play with the animals. I had a few friends who lived nearby, though I can't remember their coming to my house, and I avoided going to theirs for fear of their parents. One of the mothers used to laugh or yell at me when I didn't want to eat. Another threatened to hit me with a wooden spoon, and I was made to sit at the table until I finished. I was terrified of going there again—she made me eat tomatoes!

When I was ten years old at an annual physical exam, I thought I overheard the doctor tell my mother that I weighed too much. They said nothing to me, but after that I was conscious of my imperfect size. Salesgirls in the clothing store my mother took me to for dancing-school dresses always sympathized with my "figure problem" and recommended "A-line" skirts.

Despite my nickname, "Thunder Thighs," I wasn't obese. I weighed 142 pounds and was 5'6" tall. But I thought heavy legs and thighs were the most disgusting form of being overweight. Having a big chest still meant boys wanted to touch you, but being pear-shaped was an unspoken sin. I began to focus on my body as the source of my unhappiness. Every bite that went into my mouth was a naughty and selfish indulgence, and I became more and more disgusted with myself.

I went away to a prestigious East Coast boarding school at age fourteen. Everyone else from my grammar school class went away to private schools, too, as the local public school was considered "lower class." Without realizing how afraid I was or how to communicate my apprehensions, I left home in tears.

For months I cried at the slightest provocation. I had never approached my parents with problems and I had never confided in friends. I didn't even know what was bothering me. All I knew was that I was desperately unhappy.

The other girls at school all seemed beautiful and unapproachable: long fingernails, neat clothes, curly hair and THIN bodies. It was obvious that thin was "in" right from the start.

There were a few other girls whom I suspected had problems with food. One girl who roomed next to me for one quarter was always buying quarts of ice cream and hiding in her room. Then she would proudly announce that she was starting a diet which required fasting for the first two days. Another girl lost so much weight that her muscles could no longer hold up her 5'10" frame, and she walked bent over with her emaciated pelvis tucked forward for balance. She was taken out of school, rumored to have been throwing up all food in order to get skinny. That rumor was the first knowledge I had of someone forcibly vomiting. At that time, "bulimia" was unknown.

Even the other girl who attended the school from my hometown decided to pull a "crazy" act by eating nothing but oranges for several months. I visited her in the infirmary where she had been sent for blood sugar tests because her weight was so low, and I didn't know what to say. I secretly envied her willpower and her protruding ribs.

By the time I reached my senior year, my crying in public stopped, and I was no longer outwardly unhappy. I played sports, sang in the choir and had one good friend. She knew I thought of myself as ugly, and often reassured me that I was very pretty but I honestly thought she was humoring me like my parents did. I did my best to avoid situations which would make me feel like a failure. I begged to be let out of honors math, refused to be nominated for any offices, rarely went to dances, and was afraid to talk in class. I was happy to get cramps once a month and retreat to the safety of the infirmary. I didn't seek out many friends, and instead spent a lot of time alone or taking care of animals in the biology lab. I hoarded food in the dorm refrigerator and sometimes hid in my closet during dinner hour, sneaking food from my private stash. I kept a five-pound can of peanut butter from which I snuck teaspoonsful during the days when no one was around. Thoughts of food were often with me although I had not yet binged and purged.

I constantly tried on clothes in front of a full-length mirror to see if they had gotten looser or tighter. I took up smoking cigarettes in private, which in my mind was a bad thing to do, but it was better than eating. I chewed gum, sometimes up to five packs a day. Through all this, I managed to hold my weight steady.

Then a friend went to a doctor who gave her a diet, and she lost ten pounds in one week. Playing down my desperation, I got my mother to take me to him. He gave me a pamphlet outlining the diet, and I returned to boarding school in the spring of my senior year thinking that I was really going to change. I was going to lose the extra twenty pounds that sat between me and happiness; but the diet was horrible. I was weak and nauseous immediately. I was supposed to drink two tablespoonsful of vegetable oil before breakfast and dinner, eat only high protein foods, and drink 64 ounces of water daily. I lost eight pounds in one week, but felt bloated and nervous. Weak and sick, I went off the diet. I was a failure. At that time I had a boyfriend; but when the diet failed, I quit seeing him. I also had the word "change" in two-foot letters cut out and pasted on one wall of my room, but I no longer expected that to happen. The last months of that year were extremely painful.

I started snooping in other girls' rooms to look at their belongings. I was on a clothing allowance and never felt that I could afford anything but essentials. I sometimes "stole" things, hoarding them for a few days or weeks until the newness wore off, and then I would try to return them, unnoticed. Often an item was reported lost and there was a big to-do about how low a person the thief must be, and I would have to maneuver the circumstances so it looked as if the victim had just misplaced the missing item. I didn't want to be thought of as a thief; I just wanted to be like everyone else for a short time.

The most devastating thoughts, though, were that other people could eat and I couldn't. I would watch the skinniest, most gorgeous girl spread brown sugar and butter on her toast every morning and never get fat—never seem to feel guilty! I was jealous of everyone who was thinner than I.

The first time I thought of sticking my fingers down my throat was during the last week of school, after I saw a girl come out of the bathroom with her face all red and her eyes puffy. She had always talked about her weight and how she should be dieting even though her body was really shapely. I knew instantly what she had just done.

I tried it three weeks later in a "Wimpyburger" stand overseas. I remember the secrecy, the pain of trying and the excitement that I had found an answer to my prayers, I *could* be thin. I was spending the summer living with a Swedish farming family as an exchange student following graduation. I was afraid to decline food at any of their five daily meals! My weight got higher and higher because I couldn't always get all the food to come back up when I vomited. I was still experimenting. If a meal was dry and starchy, it would sit in my stomach and I would feel fat and bloated. During the summer, I tried to throw up at least once a day, often unsuccessfully, and left Sweden weighing 175 pounds.

I shocked everyone—including myself—by being accepted to Stanford University, 3,000 miles from home, and I left in a blatant show of independence and bravery. Once alone in my dorm room, however, I was faced with isolation and the hateful relationship I had with my Self. I retreated into eating which I knew would numb my anxiety, and I perfected the act of throwing up.

I began with breakfasts, which were served buffet-style on the main floor of the dorm. I learned which foods would come back up easily. When I woke in the morning, I often stuffed myself for half an hour and threw up before class. There were four stalls in the dorm bathroom, and I had to make sure no one caught me in the process. If it was too busy, I knew which restrooms on the way to class were likely to be empty. I always thought people noticed when I took huge portions at mealtimes, but I figured they assumed that I was an athlete and burned it off. Sometimes one meal did not satisfy the cravings, and I began to buy extra food. I always vowed that "this binge will be the last" and that I would magically and with ease metamorphose into a normal human being as soon as I threw up "this last time." I could eat a whole bag of cookies, half a dozen candy bars, and a quart of milk *on top of* a huge meal. Once a binge was under way, I did not stop until my stomach looked pregnant and I felt like I could not swallow one more time.

That year was the first of my nine years of obsessive eating and throwing up. I didn't want to tell anyone what I was doing, and I didn't want to stop. I was more attached to being numb than I was to anything else, and, although being in love or other distractions occasionally lessened the cravings, I always returned to the food.

I was convinced that bingeing was just a way to diet. There was nothing wrong with releasing tension by vomiting, even if I did it *everyday,* and I consumed tremendous quantities first. I did not consider myself addicted, and I could stop anytime, probably tomorrow.

My letters home fluctuated between questioning why I was at college and vague complaints about my health. Letter after letter said the same things: "I'm afraid, but don't worry about me." "I'm sick, but I'm being brave and getting better." "I'm probably going through some phase." Usually there was a tidbit of news at the end. With every plea for attention, there was quick reassurance that I didn't need it; and, as much as I wanted them to ask me about how alone I felt, I would have denied those feelings, I know it. I was a smart girl, had been to the best boarding school, came from a family of lawyers, bankers, and Ph.D.s. I was very athletic, seemingly independent and "together." How could I admit that I was throwing up my food to be thin?

Living with a Habit

I moved off campus in my second year because I couldn't stand the pressure of being around people all the time. I thought it looked like the kind of thing a liberated female would do, and no one questioned the move. I arranged my life to accommodate my habit, pretending to everyone, including myself, that I was being more of an adult. I vowed that when I got to the new place I would stop the eating and vomiting because I wouldn't have people around to make me nervous. I'd start an exercise program, become injected with willpower, get thin, and the world would be mine. The only hitch was that as soon as I was alone, I started bingeing and throwing up again.

I decided what I really needed was a specific weight goal. When I got there I could stop feeling like I had to diet! I chose 110 pounds because I thought I'd probably look like a model at that weight. This goal stayed with me as an eight-year obsession, and I only reached it for one day when I was dehydrated from vomiting. Even then it made no difference in my view of myself; I thought I looked the same—fat!

If I bicycled home from school, I usually carried cookies and doughnuts to eat as I pedaled. Sometimes I got home and threw up that batch only to be overwhelmed with tension an hour later, and I would set off again for an uphill ride to the grocery store. Then I could glide home downhill, cramming cookies in my mouth after the frantic, desperate ride up.

I always bought the same foods: one package of English muffins, a pound of real butter, usually a package of frozen doughnuts, a bag of Vienna finger cookies, and always milk (preferably chocolate) or ice cream—and maybe five or six candy bars to start off the binge. I would even eat waiting in line. I told the checkers that I was buying for a nursery school so they wouldn't suspect it was all for me. I could eat that much food in about an hour. If there was anything that I just couldn't finish, I threw it away, convinced and promising that this was the last time. If I hadn't bought enough food at the store, or if I was unable to get to the store at all, I would eat anything. It didn't matter. A couple of omelettes or a batch of sugar cookie dough, a loaf of toast or a whole cake.

It was different now that I was living alone. There was no worrying if the bathroom would be empty or if anyone would think it strange that I came into my room with a grocery bag full of the same foods every day. The addiction was in control.

One imagined problem—not having enough money—became a reality. My parents sent me tuition and an allowance, and I was in a work/study program testing mentally retarded children. I was happy about the work because it felt good to help others and it kept me away from food for a few hours at a time, but I always spent as much money as I earned.

It was at this point that I started stealing food. I felt a tremendous rush of independence and success when I got away with a bag of cookies or pound of butter. It was similar to my stealing at boarding school. I wanted what wasn't mine and what I felt was denied me. But there was one major difference: I did not plan on returning the goods. About six months later I was caught in a supermarket with a pint of substitute sugar in my purse, and the manager threatened me with jail. I promised to "go straight," and did, but the binges continued full force.

Marriage and a Secret Life

I had many short relationships that year which gave me attention, companionship, sex, and fun, but not what I thought was love. Then Doug, who was a friend of a friend, began to visit me and I was overwhelmed by how much I liked being with him. As we spent more time together, I could tell that he was truly a good person. Ashamed, I decided not to tell Doug about my eating habits because I was sure that they would be changing "tomorrow" anyway. I was twenty and it felt nice to be in love. Our courtship, which lasted two years, was unavoidably spent apart much of the time. When we were together for intense weekends, I would be free from the food obsessions. As soon as I graduated from college and Doug was finished with his military service, we moved in together.

We opted to look for jobs on the East Coast and stayed in an apartment over my parents' garage while we were looking. My parents fell in love with Doug even though we were unmarried and sleeping together under their roof, which made me feel that I had made a good choice. As he was included in the family, I retreated. I was used to feeling unnoticed, and I filled that emotional hole with food. While everyone else had their own projects, I was on a direct road of eating and throwing up. I lived with them but felt like an outsider, sneaking my sandwiches and cookies, and throwing up in a bathroom with a loud fan so no one could hear what I was doing. Doug and I couldn't find jobs, and after six months we moved back to California where Doug was accepted to graduate school. We also decided to get married. I never expected my eating to be a negative influence on our marriage. I didn't think it would matter that my mind was usually elsewhere, dreaming about food, because I felt loved and in love.

Daily Life

For the five years I was married to Doug, the daily rituals and idiosyncrasies of my food problems became more and more rigid. I learned to put face powder on my eyes to hide the redness from the pressure of being upside down, and on my knuckles where they got raw from rubbing against my teeth. I routinely ran water in the sink to drown out the sounds of throwing up. I got on the scale every time I passed the bathroom as well as before and after every binge. I methodically tried on my clothes in front of a full-length mirror hoping they would hang looser than the time before. I became a meticulous housekeeper, especially when I did not have a job and was "working" at home. Sometimes I delayed throwing up while I vacuumed and washed dishes, eating all the time, to set the stage for the "cleaning" of my body.

One thing I had to do between binges was run to the store to restock the food. There were days when I had to rebake batches of brownies a couple of times. I did dishes several times a day—I was averaging three to five binges every day—and I was careful to check the toilet to be sure I'd left no traces. I hoarded bulk foods. I wanted everything to be orderly and clean in the closets and on bookshelves. *The only thing that was not just perfect was me!*

I was nervous in restaurants although we ate out a lot. For nine years I never ordered an entree because I wanted to look like I was dieting. Instead, I ordered a few side dishes, but I'd suggest we get ice cream after dinner to polish off the secret binge. I always ordered whole milk, because it was thick and smooth and made the food come up easier. I even knew which restaurants had private bathrooms.

Several times I came across a book or a person or a group which I thought had meaning for me. I clung to each of these for short periods of time, but any effects were not lasting. I read books on nutrition and health, thinking they would be a positive influence. To others I seemed like a health food freak. I took a course in anatomy and physiology because I thought that if I could see what I was doing to myself physically, maybe I would stop bingeing. I was always outside myself, separate from my behavior, wanting to control it.

I was surprisingly productive in those five years. I got my B.A. from Stanford University, held two challenging jobs, and did creative projects on my own. I started a business which is still running, and I kept up relationships with family and friends, albeit from a distance.

After nine years of bingeing, however, I began to have physical side-effects, which worried me. My vision often became blurry and I had intense headaches. What used to be passing dizziness and weakness, after a few of my binges had become walking into doorjambs and exhaustion. My complexion was poor and I was often constipated. I was usually dehydrated but didn't like to drink water because it made me feel bloated. Large blood blisters appeared in the back of my mouth from my fingernails. My teeth were a mess.

Still, I refused to see that I had a serious problem even though the signs were obvious: poor health, an increasingly distant marriage, isolation, low self-esteem, fits of depression, and secrets.

Shift in Focus

In spite of the intensity of my addiction, and that I kept it all secret, Doug and I did have many happy and loving times. We never questioned being together, but he was committed to many outside activities, and I had food. When Doug got an offer for a fellowship at Cornell University, we moved back to the East Coast. I was unable to find a job there, so I decided to experiment with a batik process I had learned.

For a year I crammed my artwork between binges. I had two private showings of the batik designs, which gave me enough positive reinforcement to continue. At the end of that year, I decided to take my batiks and some soft-sculpture dolls I had made to New York City for professional feedback. I planned to stay with relatives whom I didn't know very well, which made me a little nervous, and I made appointments with designers. I tried to have confidence in my work and accept criticism willingly, but the pressure was tremendous.

Several times, I stopped at a market to pick up huge stashes of food that I devoured in my room after everyone had gone to bed. One night, preoccupied by a binge, I left my papers where I had stopped for pizza and ice cream. I ran back through dark, unfamiliar New York City streets, oblivious to the danger. My food obsession had robbed me of rational thinking!

It was on this trip that I happened upon a magazine article about people who had problems similar to mine. The article was one of the first ever written about the bingeing and vomiting cycle, and the author considered it related to anorexia nervosa, an illness characterized by self-starvation, but different because of the regular repetition of binges and purges. I was shocked! What's more, the author was conducting therapy groups five miles from where Doug and I lived!

My world suddenly shifted focus. I could not get the article out of my mind. When I returned home I spent a week bingeing heavily and then called the author, who told me to come right over. On my way, I stopped to stick my finger down my throat for what I was afraid would be the last time. What if she cured me today? I wasn't ready!

During the interview, I downplayed my lack of control and the severity of the problem. This was the first time I had told anyone! I don't know if the therapist guessed that I was holding back, but she invited me to join one of her ongoing therapy groups which would be meeting several days later. I told Doug that I had decided to deal with an old problem in a new way and added no details except that I was going for outside help. I stayed at home worrying that I would have to talk to a whole group of people about my binges.

When I got there, I presented my usual false front of confidence because I was scared to admit that I was an addict. I didn't want to say exactly how many binges a day I did, how much food I ate, how much time it took, or how alone I was most of the time—but I did. To say out loud, "I throw up five times a day," was extremely hard. The women in the group were very responsive and supportive even though each of them was struggling with her own issues. All along I had thought that I was the only person compulsively eating and vomiting, but the group helped me see that I was not alone. The therapist stressed the importance of taking actions such as speaking up, honestly acknowledging feelings, and keeping a journal. Sometimes I was able to put off binges for a day or two and I began to gain confidence that I would be able to continue getting better.

I stayed for five sessions, then Doug transferred back to Stanford. Recovering from bulimia was becoming my focus now, but I was still afraid to tell him anything. I decided that it would be a good idea for me to live alone for a while to concentrate on my cure. I told Doug that I would come to California too, but that I wanted my own place. I felt that we couldn't be together until *I had changed*. This was my addiction and I would return to him clean, pure, free, and independent when it was all behind me. He need never know.

When we got to California, we took separate places to live, which was painful and confusing for us both. We had never expected to be apart. Doug took an apartment in town, and I took a room in a house in the country. We saw each other daily, but it was always awkward. No matter what changes I felt inside, when we were together, I couldn't share them with him.

I liked Susan, the woman who owned the house where I lived, and I hoped that I could open up to her. But my bingeing began almost immediately, and I missed my group back in New York. I tried to keep up with my journal but was disgusted by my eating and wrote only about my daily life, not my feelings. Being around Stanford brought back many memories, and I returned to the same markets and doughnut shops that I used to frequent. Even though I had taken some daring steps towards curing myself, I still clung to the magical promise of getting better "tomorrow."

An art fair in Los Angeles was coming up in two months and I planned on selling my soft sculpture and batiks. I was hoping that it would be financially successful because my binges were expensive and I was running out of money. I kept on overeating and vomiting, assuming that when the fair came, things would change. I would make some money, spend some happy time with Doug, who was driving me, get some sun, and relax. I let my work on myself slide. Once again, my priority was not my cure, and I binged heavily until the fair.

Turning Point

I was really hopeful that the fair would be a turning point for me and it was, but not in a way I had expected. Monetarily it was a bust, and I sold practically nothing. By the end of the third day, I couldn't stand the thought of going back for the final day. I was a bundle of nerves and even broke down crying with Doug and his mother, with whom we were staying. I could not tell them that my greatest worries were about food, so they could not help me. I faced returning to the Bay Area to live alone, without a job, and unable to confide in anyone about the food problem that dominated my life.

It was not these aspects, though, that made the trip a turning point. It was meeting Leigh Cohn, a man who was also selling at the fair. I quickly felt close to him, and we spent hours talking when business was slow. I was conscious of his presence the entire time and did not want to say good-bye.

Within a week, Leigh and I exchanged letters and phone calls and made plans to see each other again. The attraction was incredibly strong. For three weeks, we spent almost every day together in what felt like a perfect union. Much to everyone's amazement, including our own, Leigh left an entire house of possessions in Los Angeles to live with me in my one room at Susan's so I could sell my dolls to contacts in the San Francisco Bay Area.

Doug reacted with disbelief, and we had many confrontations right from the start. My parents had been upset by our separation, but they found it incomprehensible that I was living with a man I had known for only a month. Even Susan disapproved. Everyone was against us.

Still, I felt on a very deep level that for once I was doing the right thing, and my Self blossomed in spite of the pressures. Unbelievably, the bulimia disappeared during those first weeks. Leigh and I were together almost constantly and the sudden difference in my daily routine felt wonderfully healthy and refreshing. This seemed to be that magical, instantaneous cure I had always wanted.

As the days started to follow a routine, however, my new-found strength began to fail me. I worried about the hurt I was causing my parents and Doug. I felt guilty for being so selfish. I began to question if I really was doing the right thing and if I knew my own mind! After all, I ate and vomited for nine years knowing full well I was doing something crazy; maybe I was still crazy.

As my tension increased, I began to sneak food while Leigh slept and when I was alone working at my studio. When I was bingeing, I felt numb and the doubts subsided, and I soon wanted to binge more and more. I could feel the desperation and loneliness building as it had in the past, and I was frustrated that being so completely in love hadn't completely cured me. I realized that I had a lot of work ahead if I was ever going to overcome my bulimia, and that if I didn't take the initiative then, I risked slipping permanently back into the addiction and would lose Leigh. I wanted all of my life to be as wonderful, loving, and free of bulimia as those first weeks together had been. I finally decided to take a chance and tell him, otherwise there was only secrecy and hiding. I wanted honesty and love.

The Healing Process

At first when I told Leigh about my bulimia, he thought it was not a serious problem. He had been a sweet-freak all his life, able to eat huge amounts to doughnuts and cookie dough without feeling guilty, gaining weight, or even getting cavities! He assumed that I was just a sweet-freak, too, and threw up because I felt guilty about it. As I described the size and the frequency of my binges, however, he could tell how desperate I was. It was a tearful, emotional outburst. He was compassionate, listened well, and resolved to help me.

I had always expected to get better *tomorrow,* but this time I knew that I had to start taking definite steps *now.* I made two resolutions. I would be absolutely honest and tell Leigh about all binges, and I would do anything to cure myself—even be locked away in a sanitarium or some unknown treatment facility if necessary. Leigh promised to stick by me as long as I stayed committed to my cure. He helped me come up with ideas about what actions I could take, listened, supported, laughed, and loved me; but we understood that I had to stop the bingeing by myself.

We made lists: immediate goals, future goals, what to do when alone instead of bingeing, things that were changing in my life, "Poor-Lindsey and Lucky-Lindsey" lists, what I liked and disliked about myself, how I felt about my parents, etc. I prepared a checklist of things I could do if I was on the verge of a binge. I did one item at a time until I overcame the desire to eat. Some of the diversions were to exercise, sew, garden, take a walk, or soak in a hot bath. The last thing on the list was to contact Leigh or another friend and talk about my feelings. I used this method about a dozen times and it worked well.

There were several new activities that I wanted to incorporate into my daily life. I didn't do all of these things every day, but I tried to be as consistent as possible. I began meditating regularly and started writing in my journal again. I tried to establish a positive frame of mind and feel more relaxed. I decided to drink a certain amount of water each day, but I had a hard time with that so I revised my expectations rather than feel like a failure. I also decided, at Leigh's suggestion, that I allow myself one "forbidden" treat daily without guilt. This was a completely different way to eat and surprisingly easy.

One major step I took, which is in the "junk food" category, requires a special preface. Although this activity had a tremendous impact on my confidence, to do it alone would have invited failure. No one should try this without support and supervision. Having said that, I'll describe an all-day binge I did with Leigh to prove that I didn't have to vomit. On the big day, I woke up to a bag of malted milk balls on the bedside table, which Leigh had gotten to start the binge *right*! We bought a pound of candy, a dozen doughnuts, caramel apples, caramel corn, a batch of homemade cookies, brownies, and drinks—all to take with us in the car on a business trip we had to take to San Francisco. During the course of the day we also ate hamburgers and fries, milkshakes, a greasy meal of fish and chips, and an all-day-long continuous dessert of white chocolate. By bedtime, we were both exhausted and stuffed. Leigh felt sick, but I was preoccupied by how my body looked and felt. I looked pregnant and I couldn't lie down comfortably in any position. In spite of all this discomfort, I was actually quite proud of myself. I laughed at this incredible stunt I had accomplished. Leigh would not let me out of his sight for obvious reasons. I would never have tried this without a support person; undoubtedly, I would have vomited.

The next day we fasted, which was almost as frightening to me as it had been to binge the entire day before. But, after keeping in so much "junk food," I wanted my system to rest. Fasting turned out not to be as difficult as I had feared and I got hungry again by evening. I was sure I had gained weight, but I hadn't, and that made me even more confident. This was a real turning point for me—I knew I could reach a goal, and I had power over food.

I began reading books that I thought might help me learn more about my inner-self. I learned specific exercises I could do that enabled me to be more objective about some of my values and beliefs as well as my parents and childhood. I also read books about spir-

ual masters whose lives inspired me to be more loving
owards myself and others.

When Leigh and I were first living together, I began
o see a psychiatrist because of the tension and guilt I
elt living with Leigh while still married to Doug. I
idn't mention my bulimia at first, but when I did tell
im, he recommended that I see a woman psychiatrist
who had treated anorexics. At that time, bulimia was
still virtually unknown by most people. I saw her once,
ut we did not relate well. I realized the importance of
onfiding in someone, however, and decided to con-
nue using Leigh.

The most difficult thing that I had to do was to tell
eople the truth all the time. I started by sharing my
ulimia with the people I least wanted to. Doug, who
ad finally accepted our separation as permanent, took
y confiding as a genuine act of caring, and felt sad-
ened by what I had been through. He was surprised
nd sympathetic; he said he didn't know why he hadn't
sked me about why I was in the bathroom so much. I
ink we were closer after that than we had been in
ears.

About a month later, I substituted letter writing for
ournal entries. I always left open the option of not
ending them or sending a revised copy. I wrote my
arents letters that explained what I was going
hrough, but did not ask for or expect much participa-
on from them. I also talked to my brothers and sis-
rs who have confronted many of the same issues.
ur conversations often gave me support because I
as able to observe in them traits of my own, and they
emed okay!

I began to confide in friends. Most were interested,
mpathetic, and supportive, though a few dropped out
f my life. I wrote the following in a letter to my

childhood friend, the one who had eaten all thos
oranges at boarding school: "Finally I can tell peopl
about eating and throwing up and not be ashamed. D
you know how ashamed I have been all these year
thinking I was abnormal and disgusting?"

Even when I wasn't bingeing, I was thinking abou
food most of the time, and this was very frustrating fo
me. I had a lot of pent-up energy that I needed t
release in ways other than bingeing. So Leigh and
wrestled on a large foam mattress on the floor and ha
exhausting fights with foam bats. I punched a boxin
bag we had in our garage, and took long saunas. When
needed to, I screamed into a pillow until I was hoarse
All these things had a settling effect on my mind a
well as my body.

During these months, I grew more comfortable wit
just being myself. I had always been desperate to main
tain an image of unfailing perfection and independenc
but now I stopped hiding my shyness, my anger, an
my fears. Finally, as I grew to understand who I wa
and why, I also understood how well the bulimia ha
served me. It had been my friend, my buffer, my se
curity, and my expression when I knew no other. As a
addiction, however, it was allowing no other behavio
but itself, and had taken me over. I fought hard to ge
me back!

The binges gradually diminished in number and size
During the first few months, I did several, but the
dwindled to one every couple of months. When I di
occasional binges, I considered them setbacks bu
used them to better understand why I binged and wha
I would do the next time to stop myself.

During the first six months of recovery, I pushe
myself to do my program. Whatever were the cause
for my bulimia—some I understood but others surel

escaped me—my priority was living without it rather than trying to figure it out. Facing torturous cravings to binge and successfully replacing them had me on an emotional rollercoaster; but, little by little, the struggle got easier.

I Made It!

There came a point when days could go by without any thoughts of bingeing. I began to enjoy eating, cooking, and going to restaurants. After all of my perseverance, positive thinking had become more of a habit than a practice. At one point, I baked a cake for a couple of friends who were coming for dinner. They knew about my bulimia, and asked me how I could now make a cake without eating the whole thing. I told them that I forced myself to concentrate on the joy of the meal to come instead of feeling bad in any way. I wanted to be able to bake, just like anyone else, and it really wasn't that hard anymore.

My self-image was transforming. I began to think of myself as a funny, loving, successful, positive-minded person. If doubts crept up on me, I trusted that I was doing the right thing. Even being alone was enjoyable.

My social life underwent drastic changes. I made a conscious effort to resolve any conflicts left over from past relationships, and even rekindled some old friendships. In the past, I had made excuses to avoid being around people, but now I found that some of my happiest moments were with Leigh, my siblings, and friends. Although my parents did not actively participate in my recovery, they knew about it and did ask how I was doing. We became much closer. Doug and I divorced, but remained interested in and supportive of each other. I wasn't afraid of people anymore.

When business commitments ended in San Francisco, Leigh and I moved to Santa Barbara, away from the old haunts. We got married and continued to spend most of our time together. At first, a lot of our effort was spent on recovery; but, as that progressed, we focused more on my growing soft-sculpture business. We worked full-time with a staff, opened a retail store filled with my dolls, and expanded our wholesale market to more than 300 stores throughout the United States. I truly loved my life and respected who I had become.

A year and a half after I made the decision to stop, I considered myself "cured." Then Leigh and I wrote a pamphlet called *Eat Without Fear,* thinking that putting my bulimia on paper would be the final purge. My bingeing and vomiting were indeed over, but my involvement with eating disorders education was only beginning. I started getting letters from bulimics who were inspired to quit by *Eat Without Fear.* I was the first bulimic to talk about her own story on national television. Newspaper and magazine articles, some about me, began to appear. Public awareness about bulimia grew. We started giving lectures and workshops, wrote more about bulimia, and talked to many, many people who wanted to overcome their own food problems. We fell into an inspirational, educational role, which also became our business.

I'm gratified by the contributions I've made in this field, especially to those individuals who have been inspired by me to change. I certainly didn't expect to be in the role that I am, but since the start of my healing, little miracles have presented themselves; and, as I chose to notice them, they led me in this direction. I've followed my heart and gotten true nourishment—love.

Overcoming Bulimia

Where to Start

The Decision to Stop

Each time I did a binge, I swore that it would be my last. I told myself, "Tomorrow I'll quit cold turkey." Though I made these promises thousands of times in the nine years I spent bingeing and vomiting, I ignored the fact that I was addicted. I also expected that one day the "right" book, diet, or man would make my cravings magically disappear, and then—presto—so would any other problems. I sort of wanted to end the bulimia; but, for many years, I took no action to stop. I resisted making any decisions that committed me to getting better. Instead, I waited for a transformation to occur. When I first read about bulimia, I was shocked to learn that there were other people with similar fears, rituals, and secrets that revolved around food. When I discovered there was a name for my "disease" and that people could get over it, I took my first serious steps towards recovery.

Bulimia will continue indefinitely, unless a decision is made to finally end it. I advocate choosing not to binge for many reasons: to live a longer, healthier, more loving life, to enjoy eating, to have honest relationships, reach potentials of creativity, save money . . . The list is endless. It does not really matter what the reasons are, just that commitment be combined with action.

Rarely, and never without some struggle, is a cure instantaneous. It takes bravery to confront addictive behavior, the first steps being the most difficult. After all, bulimia is serving to protect us from sadness, anxiety, boredom, spiritual emptiness, and other painful feelings. To give up that protection is scary; we are alone with an uncertain future. Several bulimics we surveyed pointed out that they were "experts" on nutrition, health, and psychology. They understood on an intellectual level that their compulsive eating was unhealthy, but understandably still resisted making the commitment to change. All but three percent of the bulimics who responded said that they wanted to stop bingeing. In each of the cases where a recovery was sought, there was an initial decision to change:

I've spent the last six months accumulating information on stopping bulimic behavior. However I've avoided doing anything concrete—avoided taking control of my recovery. Up until last week I've been waiting for that magic day when the bingeing stops—each binge would be my last ever. Now hesitantly, shakily, I'm making a start.

Realizing that I am the only person who could stop my behavior helped me start my cure. I finally understood that neither God nor my mother could automatically cure me. It was all up to me.

Really, it was the decision to stop that did it. Then, I had to be quite forgiving to myself and give up my need to be perfect. As I began to eat better, I started eating less crap and craving less junk. It took me two years to stop craving food. I binge on occasion, but I have been symptom-free for four years.

What has helped in my cure is seeking that cure. I became willing to try anything to find the combination of things that worked for me.

Different factors lead to the decision to stop. A twenty-eight-year-old woman who binged seven times daily wrote:

Self-education on bulimia has helped. I was bulimic for thirteen years without knowing others had it. That knowledge and the knowledge that the author of Eat Without Fear *had actually recovered from the same illness helped me the most.*

Several bulimics mentioned experiences of physical complications, such as:

An experience that made a big difference to me was a near-death situation from poor physical health due to numerous daily bulimic episodes. I contracted malnutrition, double pneumonia, a spastic colon, and hypoglycemia. I was finally hospitalized for three weeks. Following my hospitalization, I got involved in an eight-week group therapy, which met four days a week for six hours daily.

Fear! My hospitalization was not premeditated or planned. It was emergency hospitalization for cardiac problems from low potassium. Afterwards, I quit "overnight" and never went back to vomiting, but it was very difficult psychologically.

This twenty-eight-year-old bulimic, who was also anorexic and vomited once or twice daily for ten years, was hospitalized with dangerously low levels of potassium from vomiting. After receiving potassium intravenously, she began to feel immediate relief from physical distress, and continued taking potassium supplements for nine months, while going "cold turkey" without binges. After she started to feel better, she became more capable of understanding and changing her behavior:

Vomiting destroys not only your digestive health but also the feedback mechanisms that produce the signals of satisfaction after a meal. If your system does not get the calories and nutrients it asks for via hunger signals, it will continue to ask for them. Although this may sound simplistic, it had significance for me. I had to become reacquainted with my body's signals. I had to face the terrifying fear of retaining the food after a binge. I found that my body did not self-destruct. Although it was painful to keep down the food, I found that the next day, my hunger was greatly reduced. This was not a matter of willpower; I simply was not hungry. To my surprise, this did not produce long-term weight gain, although there were short-term fluctuations in my weight. (And note: I do not have a high metabolism.) However, I faced the fact that I would never be able to maintain as low a weight as I wished if I was to give up the bulimia. Hunger at a reasonable weight is different than hunger at an unreasonably low weight.

However, the mere knowledge of side-effects did not guarantee that a bulimic would stop. A bulimic nurse described her physical problems in quite specific medical terms, yet hid this information from doctors who were also her friends. A thirty-eight-year-old woman who spent thousands of dollars on dental work during fifteen years of vomiting felt fortunate that the damage to her body was not worse. Twenty-two percent of the bulimics that answered the survey were hospitalized for their symptoms. Interestingly, few of them categorized that experience as "most helpful." This thirty-two-year-old, who has been bulimic for about three years, knew what the physical side-effects were, but that was not enough to "cure" her.

I try to scare myself about my health—that if I binge and vomit one more time I will surely die, choke to death, have cardiac arrest, or my teeth will fall out. Sometimes this works but it is usually in remorse after a binge—not before. I don't talk about this subject with anyone. My therapist only mentioned it once after I brought it up, and it took forever to bring up the subject because I was so embarrassed.

The dramatic changes in body weight and appearance which occur during pregnancy affected several women's behavior in differing ways, often prompting them to stop:

I had a premature baby who lived three weeks. My doctors said my bulimic behavior prior to the pregnancy had nothing to do with the premature delivery. I'm sure, though, that fourteen years of bulimia, in one form or another, had a great deal of impact on my body's ability to handle pregnancy. I thought this experience would be enough to "cure me forever," however, about three weeks after he died, I began to return to old habits.

I miscarried and then my bulimia returned for about a month, but I got my priorities straight and have been good. I am again pregnant and I do not want to lose this baby, so at least for nine months I will be eating normally. I'm almost too strict with myself because I am so afraid.

I try harder than ever to overcome it because I'm expecting my first child and am conscious of what I eat for the baby's sake. As soon as I eat something fattening or high in calories, I vomit. I know it isn't good for me or the baby. My husband thinks that since I'm pregnant I've overcome it, but I haven't. I need help! I have gained some weight, but not a lot. The doctors aren't worried, so I'm not either. I have a lively baby kicking inside of me right now.

My bulimic/anorexic behavior has ceased almost entirely because I'm pregnant. I'm not suggesting pregnancy as a solution, but a deep caring feeling toward others can sometimes set you on the road to recovery.

The experience that made the biggest difference in my cure was becoming pregnant and giving birth. Having a baby changed my view of my identity where one had previously been lacking or camouflaged in my body shape and desire for thinness. The role of my body took on a new perspective. The externally motivated desire to be thin—fitting into some societal prescription for beauty and happiness—was no longer in my reach.

This gave me an opportunity to find or feel my own standards and to question "theirs" from my new, non-competitive, pregnant perspective. I do not advocate pregnancy as a cure, but it happened at the right time for me.

Once I decided to get better, I trusted myself and remained persistent, even though I often wanted to run to the refrigerator for help. As my fears gradually subsided, I began to have an increased sensitivity to and love for my world, which many recovering bulimics also describe. If you feel like you are fighting an uphill battle, keep in mind that your life as a bulimic is worse. When I committed myself to recovery, I was willing to do anything. YOU are worth the time and effort that it takes. YOU can cure yourself! YOU can have a happy life. Look in the mirror everyday, and congratulate yourself for taking the initiative to make your life work.

Setting Reasonable Goals

One strategy that came up repeatedly was to work within a framework of success rather than failure. In this manner, positive thoughts replaced negative ones, setback binges were opportunities to better understand the compulsion, and successes were rewarded with praise, happier feelings, and tangible results.

We received a survey response from one of the first women to read *Eat Without Fear*. She had been anorexic and then bulimic for twelve of her twenty-eight years. At first, she was relieved to read that someone else who was bulimic had "gotten well," and she went several days without bingeing. She then opened up to her husband, who was supportive, and she entered professional therapy. She now considers herself "cured" and wrote this quote about her early progress:

In the beginning, I had to make very deliberate decisions to do something else—to fight off an urge that I knew would only come back to haunt me again. I had to accept that each time I decided not to throw up was an experience that I could add to my repertoire of getting better. This allowed me to accept any failures because these failures never subtracted from my "getting better times." A failure did not mean all was lost. I could not throw up next time. At those times I would use the failures to examine the circumstances that led me to throw up. From this I could learn to avoid certain circumstances. At first, I thought this was weak, that I "should" be able to face anything to really be getting better. But I also had to face that I needed to build up my repertoire of holding in food so I could get stronger, and if that meant playing games with myself, that was OK. I became more self-accepting which enabled me to feel better about myself. I began to carefully examine how I felt after I had thrown up and also how I felt when I didn't. I gained greater trust in myself and in my ability to get well if I chose to.

Not a single survey indicated that a "cure" was immediate. In every case, recovery meant taking action, enduring pressures, and having some binges in the early stages. Many shared that they tried to set reasonable goals, and some experimented with keeping simple contracts.

Basically, being willing to go through a whole hell of a lot of emotional pain and suffering has helped me the most. I make small, achievable goals, rather than overwhelming ones. Gradually, I have gone from seven times a day to once or maybe twice a week.

I plan my day and stick to the schedule, not allowing myself to "play it by ear" and panic at the first moment I feel alone or hungry or unoccupied. It isn't regimented, it's guided. I set small goals and achieve them. I use a checklist.

I'm trying not to be obsessed with curing overnight. I know it takes time! Now I'm stopping after less and less food ingested than previous binges—two bagels instead of six. My therapist calls it "discreet amounts." My binges have lessened greatly. They used to be my whole day, my whole life. Now, I am trying to look to the future when it won't be so all important. I can see it progressing to this and feel great about that progress. Self-love really helps, and also not giving up. There's always tomorrow.

It was less difficult to make a very small amount of progress each day, taking a step at a time, than trying to improve everything all at once.

I stop myself from bingeing by recalling the pain experienced after bingeing; and, instead I do something positive for myself even when feeling depressed. Then I really "get into" feeling good about what I've done. This took me a long time to get to. I took baby steps the whole way!

I used to give myself stars for every day I completed without throwing up. I bought the shiny colored stars like I got in grade school. For some reason, this *worked. Another time I would put $.50 in a jar for each day I completed and saved up for something I wanted.*

With more repeated successes at being able to stop, I have a greater sense of control.

Don't panic if nothing you've tried has worked yet. It's a battle you are fighting and it's hard to win each time. If you decide to stop the bulimic habit, you've got to expect occasional setbacks. Don't be too hard on yourself, but don't fool yourself either.

The biggest step for me was to stop throwing up if I binged. I'm at the point where I'll binge once in a while but at least I find comfort in knowing I've come so much farther than last year! And next year I'll be even better!

4

Get Support!

The struggle to overcome eating disorders is much easier with outside support. This can come from many different people, not only trained professionals. When bulimics say that I am the first person they told, I always encourage them to seek out a "next" person to tell. One woman enlisted the support of everyone on her dormitory floor. She made a public statement about her problem and asked that they all help her to stop bingeing. They responded in full force!

Bulimics have often mentioned that they are afraid that their husbands, lovers, parents, roommates, or others will catch them bingeing or vomiting. They are embarrassed and afraid to tell the truth. They also develop resentments towards those people from whom they are hiding. In my case, I resented my family tremendously for the times they never asked what I was doing in the bathroom, even though I would only have said, "Oh, I'm okay," and excluded them. I was afraid to tell them anything or accept support.

When I was eventually able to tell Leigh, I found him surprised, sympathetic and supportive. We made a deal that I would tell him every time I binged, and we would discuss it. In a short time, I would tell him when I felt like bingeing instead of actually doing it. If he was not available, I tried to call another friend, wrote in my journal, or did some other activity (more on these later).

For most bulimics, being honest by giving up all of the secrecy and pretence is usually frightening, as well as a tremendous relief. Bingeing and purging takes a lot of energy, and so does keeping it secret! Eighty-five percent of the bulimics surveyed acknowledged that secrecy was one of the most difficult obstacles to overcome, but their comments indicated the value of being truthful:

Certainly I feel secretive about this habit because I view it as disgusting as well as socially unacceptable. No one else knows.

Coming out of the closet and talking to people has probably been most helpful.

A bulimic lifestyle is inundated with lies. Lying became so much a part of me, it was difficult to remember what was truth. Lies involving food, stealing, etc. carried over to lying about everything. I figured that if I told the truth and admitted my imperfection, I'd be in trouble. For me, breaking free meant always telling the truth and accepting myself like that—imperfect, but fully human.

I strongly urge telling the family and friends about bulimia. It's difficult to conquer alone.

Telling my husband after four years has helped me the most. He is supportive and I don't hate myself as much anymore because I'm not lying to him. Talking about it to family members and a therapist has helped a lot too.

Telling my husband has helped me the most, all the secrecy was the hardest thing to cope with.

Family Support

There's no denying that we are affected by our families, both genetically and socially. Even if we leave home, we bring attitudes and habits to our new environments. We often relate to food and to each other in the same ways as our parents and siblings. Whether you choose to include your family in your recovery or not, it is important to recognize how they have influenced you, and decide what to do about it.

If you look at your family members, you'll probably see that you share many physical features. Your mother may have the same fat thighs that your grandmother had, and if fat thighs bother you, you may be horrified to look in the mirror and see that you are filling out just like them. It may seem even worse if Mom is unhappy about her size. She may be unable to change her values, but you must. Part of ending your bulimia is accepting that you have been born prone to a certain body type. Your shape can be altered by the amount of food you eat and the amount of exercise you get, but what's the point? Obsessing about looks you inherited is fruitless.

Children learn most of their social skills in the home. Parents serve as examples for coping skills, attitudes, and eating habits, and set ideals of ambition, perfection, and acceptance. Although they may not mean to disapprove or discourage individual growth, their actions often send conflicting statements. For example, a child may be told not to eat before dinner, yet may see mother sneaking spoonfuls as she cooks. Parents establish rules and myths for us. Some are direct, like: no dessert unless you eat everything on your plate; growing boys need to eat more than girls; or father always gets served first. Others are less obvious, like: emotions should be expressed by yelling; misbehavior is best disciplined authoritatively rather than with rational discussion; or boys can be trusted to stay out late, while girls are less responsible and must come home early. For bulimics, leaving home does not mean instant recovery, because those learned behaviors are carried along.

Overall, 91% of the bulimics surveyed felt that their families contributed to their eating disorder. For some, realizing their family's impact made it possible for them to turn to them for support; but, many bulimics said that their families could not relate to food problems, because they either ate "normally" or were also obsessed. Meals were often scenes of confrontation or hidden pain and resentment. Some expressed fear that loved ones would find their behavior repulsive, and others used their bulimia as a way of getting back at their families. In any case, the behavior was an added problem and in no way improved the relationships.

Family therapy coupled with assertiveness training can be extremely helpful, especially when the bulimic is living at home. Some therapists require that the family be treated as a whole. This is because the methods of communication in these families are often ineffective and can be greatly improved by learning new skills. Ideally, this would be acknowledged by all family members, and improving their relationships would be a shared commitment. However, you might decide not to involve your family at all, because they may be too unapproachable or unwilling to attempt change. It is still helpful, though, to acknowledge their influence and perhaps open up to them.

Here are some reflections:

Loved ones could not have helped me at all. I feel that my family was 95% of the cause. My mother and her entire family is obsessed with cooking, eating, and people's weights.

Moving away from my family helped, because I got away from their constant criticism and judging of me. My parents always made me feel as though I wasn't really my own person, but rather a reflection of themselves. All of the neighbors and relatives would surely be watching to see how I turned out. Mom and Dad's success or failure would be judged, so I had to be perfect.

My bulimia has decreased almost ninety percent and I have my parents to thank for that. They have been very supportive and are always there when I need help.

I have difficulty getting support from my family, especially admitting to them that I need the help and asking for it, since I have always been the one to help and support others.

My mother is a help because she is there when I need someone, but I have to admit sometimes she hurts me deeply as I don't feel she loves me unconditionally. Our relationship is better when I'm doing well than when I'm having problems, and that's when I need her support the most.

The biggest help in my cure was the Sunday night reports I would give my mom. After an entire week without bingeing or purging I told my mom about my accomplishment. I could see the relieved expression on her face, and that was enough to get me through any rough spots I encountered through the week. As each week went by it became increasingly easier to not throw up. Whole days went by without even a thought of vomiting.

While I lived at my mother's home, I always felt that I had to give up the bulimia for the sake of the people I lived with. This was not enough motivation.

They were helpful while it lasted, but my parents gave up when I would have a relapse. Now, I feel as though they don't care, like I'm a lost cause.

My mother has been absolutely no help at all, and the few times I have opened up to her, she has not been willing to understand, but just laughs the whole thing off and tells me I shouldn't worry about getting fat.

My parents can't conceive of my personal turmoil, so I don't even bother trying to reach out to them. I only end up feeling hurt, rejected, and resentful of their inability to empathize with my pain. I have enough to deal with without all that anger too.

This thirty-eight-year-old has been bulimic for twenty-two years:

My family does not know I am bulimic. I am still afraid to tell them.

There has been a vast improvement in how I regard my parents. Hatred is replaced by love and understanding on my part. A show of more genuine affection is now shown by them. All of us are more honest.

If you are a family member, do not coerce the bulimic into therapy with the belief that you are immune to counseling. You might play an active part in her history and recovery. Be ready to take a deep look at yourself and your own coping patterns.

When recovering bulimics are considering the affects of their family, there is a lifetime worth of observations. Examining their contribution to the cause of your bulimia is one thing, enlisting their support in the present cure is another. Remember that deep within you all is a natural, common, unconditional love for each other, regardless of who they are or how you have related in the past. Be truthful with them, and let them help you as much as they can. (Show them our "Specific Advice for Loved-Ones.")

Professional Therapy

Most bulimics agree that talking about their food problems is extremely difficult, but a tremendous relief. Professional therapists are excellent choices for this kind of support, because that is their profession. While bulimics may be embarrassed to "tell all" to a friend or family member, especially at the beginning of recovery, a therapist has no investment in seeing them as "perfect." One feeling that a few individuals expressed was that no one other than a bulimic could truly understand the pain. While this may be true, professional therapists are trained and paid to listen, empathize, and provide coping skills. Also, therapists are objective. They offer guidance, acceptance, and knowledge about self-discovery. They will fully "be there" for their client and this is crucial for overcoming those feelings of loneliness and disgust which tend to perpetuate bulimia. We strongly recommend that all bulimics seek out some professional therapy.

There are many kinds of therapists and therapy techniques used for treating bulimia and anorexia nervosa. It is important to find the "right" therapist as well as approach. Some professionals are specifically trained and certified to treat people with eating disorders. Others may have taken courses in addictions or treated many patients with eating disorders. Although it is difficult to "interview" therapists it is essential to find one with whom you feel comfortable. Some women stated that they had seen five or six different therapists before finally finding one who helped them. Remember, "therapist" is a vague term which most often refers to psychiatrists, psychologists, or marriage and family counselors; but, other professionals might also be excellent counselors, such as: licensed social workers, nutritionists, school counselors, clergymen, acupuncturists, hypnotists, chiropractors, and others. Some types of therapy are: individual sessions, group sessions specifically centered on bulimia, groups with various types of eating disorders or issues, or family therapy. The lengths of treatment vary from a few sessions to several years. (Re-read the answers about professional therapy in the "Questions Most Often Asked About Bulimia" chapter.)

Professional therapy received the highest praise on the surveys. Eighty percent found it helpful, and it was rated "most help" much more often than any other category. These comments represent the feelings of many other bulimics who also wrote about therapy:

Locating the right therapist for me was the most important element. Involvement in a self-help group was valuable.

I saw many different therapists, from psychiatrists to non-credentialed counselors, but the last therapist I saw was the only one that helped me!

My therapist has helped me to look at many aspects of myself that I was either unconscious of, or that I had pushed aside because they were too painful for me to deal with.

I highly recommend professional therapy. It has brought tremendous insight into my eating disorder.

Seeing my psychotherapist by myself and at times with my mom has been the best help to me.

The thing that has helped me the most is my group therapy. It enables me to see others with the same problem, and is the only place I feel I can be honest with myself and others about my problem.

One of my teachers recommended I go to the counseling center at school. This was the best move I could have made. My counselor has been very helpful. She has helped me talk about feelings and anxieties which were being ignored or substituted for by my eating.

The most effective treatment which I have experienced was working with a team of a psychologist who was experienced with bulimic patients and a dietitian. We begin working on a goal-driven plan adding a new goal each week. Through this plan, I progressed from purging every time I ate to keeping down up to sixteen meals!

Eating Disorder Treatment Centers

There are many hospitals and clinics that have special eating disorder treatment programs. An increasing number of these facilities are opening all the time. Most offer in-patient and out-patient services. Typically, these centers employ a multi-dimensional approach to treating anorexics and bulimics. They usually have a team of skilled professionals including: a medical director who is often certified in psychiatry, a program director, a psychologist who specializes in eating disorders, licensed clinical social workers or marriage and family counselors, a registered dietitian, plus a well-rounded medical and nursing staff. Treatment often includes individual and group therapy sessions, nutritional counseling, assertiveness training, relaxation and exercise programs, and sometimes the use of drugs.

Regardless of where you live, there are probably treatment centers nearby. In metropolitan areas, their advertisements are easily found in the media. Consult your local hospitals to see what programs they offer. Additionally, you might get referrals from the eating disorder organizations which are listed in the Resources section.

Other Support

Support was found by the survey members in many kinds of relationships ranging from close friends to support groups. A few women described the value they placed on the unconditional love of pets, ranging from horses to dogs to fish! Free help can usually be found by contacting local college health or counseling centers who may have on-going support groups. Many hospitals and individual therapists also sponsor free or low-cost groups that are open to the public.

Another no cost option that has worked for many people is Overeaters Anonymous. Most communities have OA chapters, and many have groups specifically for bulimics. Check your local telephone listings for a list of meeting times and places. Their national headquarters is also listed along with other eating disorders organizations in the Resources section of this book.

We stress that it is up to you to take action! There IS support if you look hard enough. We state this again and again, because it is so important, as these quotes indicate:

The biggest key I've found is expressing myself and reaching out to others for help. In talking with other bulimics and asking people to listen to me, I gain a sense of who I am, relief from anxiety and anger and a secure feeling that I am okay. Today I have over seven months of no vomiting, part of which I believe is a spiritual miracle, and part is my willingness to show others who I really am.

The fact that most people close to me were not repulsed by me for my behavior made a big difference.

Reaching out to others when I have felt like bingeing has helped me get through those times.

I felt a lot less isolated after opening up and baring my

soul to two trusted girlfriends. Their prayers and undying support meant a lot. I learned that I was not unacceptable as a person, even if I did have an eating disorder I hated.

I had a friend call me every night and I would tell her how I did. Knowing I was going to talk to her helped me to make the decision earlier not to throw up.

The biggest help to me has been having people around to "guard" and "babysit" me. They kept me away from food and showed me how to "act normally" around food.

I encourage group support, many heads together give different insights to problems.

Talking to my friend, who was anorexic and bulimic for eight years and is recovered for three, is always helpful.

Any support group where people share their honest feelings is helpful. Isolation is the bulimic's greatest enemy.

Seeing other bulimics who were recovering gave me hope that I could recover.

I have done a dozen or more things that were attacks on my compulsive eating, and I can point to aspects of each that have been valuable to me: the nutritional information from Weight Watchers, the comraderie and spiritual focus of Overeaters Anonymous, the increased self-esteem and general living strategies from counseling and growth experiences, the surrender and letting go from spiritual awareness, and the continual

*support from someone close to me who knew my se-
cret, horrible behavior.*

Although many women described difficulty opening
up to their husbands or lovers, the response they received was usually very supportive and helpful. One
response to *Eat Without Fear* came from this twenty-
eight-year-old who has binged up to five times daily for
the last year and a half and has used many types of
purges:

*Your booklets are terrific, but what do those people do
who aren't as lucky to have supportive people like
Leigh?*

Our answer has always been that the support can
come from anyone who is willing to participate in the
recovery by being honest, positive, and encouraging
(see "Specific Advice for Loved Ones"). Just as
therapists are professionally responsible to give support, husbands and lovers are morally responsible to
help; and, most of them do an excellent job! These
examples are a small selection of many similar remarks:

*The most important factor in my recovery has been the
support of someone who loves me unconditionally,
in spite of who I am and the ugliness of my problem.
My husband now, boyfriend during many of the years
of my bulimia, did not reject or leave me when he
found out about my vomiting. He also never lectured
me about giving it up. He did not, however, shield me
from the truth of the physiological danger from my
actions. In fact, he told me that I would most likely die
from some direct or indirect effect of my bulimia if I*

did not give it up. The way he put it, though, made it clear that whether or not I did so, I would be doing it mostly for my own benefit—although clearly he would benefit, too. He told me later that he had thought over all the approaches he could have taken with me and came up with the only possible one he could. It required tremendous restraint at times, especially when he was filled with worry for me.

My husband helped me greatly by being very uncritical. His feelings of love and acceptance took the pressure off. Telling him when I failed, allowed me to deeply experience my sadness yet know I was still loved. Somehow I felt he had faith in my ability to recover. I felt he understood the magnitude of the difficulty involved in recovery. One practical thing I requested of him was to inquire how I was doing, because I knew that if he was going to ask me how I did that day, I would not want to tell him I had thrown up.

My husband has helped tremendously by not mentioning the behavior even when he's aware it's occurred. He is always willing to let me talk about it when I need to, but doesn't pry or probe or bring it up.

I am very fortunate to have a husband who loves me. He's tough on me sometimes and doesn't pity me when I'm feeling sorry for myself, but he is very honest with me. He's a good sounding board.

An important factor is having someone love me and being able to really feel and believe in that love. I never felt anyone could really love me, even though they said the words, I guess since I hated myself so much, I couldn't see why they could love me.

Medical and Dental Examinations

If you are bulimic, it is likely that you have done some harm to your body. For this reason, you should have a complete physical examination from a physician, who is familiar with bulimia, and who will encourage you to care for your body.

The secretive nature of this addiction kept the medical profession in the dark for a long time. Fortunately, most doctors are now familiar with its symptoms and side-effects. Be sure yours is. If not, ask for a referral from a local treatment facility or therapist who specializes in eating disorders.

Sometimes doctors are intimidating because of their time constraints and implied stature. But be assertive. Do not make excuses to avoid a physical examination. The cost is no more than a few binges, and in most areas there are clinics available with sliding fees. Be sure to tell the doctor your complete bulimic history. It is important to be honest.

It is also important to have a dental check-up, expecially if you vomit. Stomach acid removes tooth enamel, and constant exposure to food, especially sugar, causes serious tooth and gum decay. My teeth were an absolute mess for years, and have cost me thousands of dollars worth of dental work, but I have not had a single cavity since I stopped bingeing.

5

What Has Worked for Many

Recovering bulimics need to develop new, healthier habits. They are exploring unfamiliar and often scary territory. As uncomfortable as this feels at first, it's like starting any new venture. It becomes easier with time, and rewarding on different levels. If you are starting a recovery, there are many suggestions for you in this chapter. Think about each of them as they relate to you, and try them over and over until they become your new way of being.

Acceptance

There is a saying which goes, "What you resist, persists." If you have an eating disorder, there is a strong possibility that you are resisting something in your life or within yourself which is manifesting itself through your behavior. It might be a hurt that happened a long time ago, something someone did to you, or vice versa, a belief which causes you low self-esteem, or something about your present circumstances which upsets you. Whatever it is, resisting the memory of it, the reality of it, and the feeling of it gives it life in some aspect of your bulimia.

The fact is that there are some things you can change and some things you can't. You can't change your heredity, your past, or the fact that you are human and are therefore not perfect. And for the most part, you can't change other people or circumstances. So, what is left? YOU. *You* can change your attitude and perspective towards life. The practice of acceptance and forgiveness is the easiest, most effective place to start.

It might seem as though accepting ourselves and our situations will just perpetuate the status quo and diminish any motivation for self-improvement. However, the opposite is true. Practicing acceptance lets you see more clearly. Practicing acceptance takes the pressure off so you can see realistically what you are able and willing to change. It helps make clear the fact that you do have choices.

The emphasis here is on practice. This means you have to take the initiative. For example, if you have always resisted loving your parents for whatever reason, practice visualizing them surrounded by your feelings of love. If you have made mistakes in the past, try to see them as the best that you could do at the time. Even setback binges are opportunities to learn how your bulimia is serving you rather than proof of your weakness. If you hate your body, talk to it in the mirror, dialoguing with those lumps and bumps. How much will it realistically change? Breathe love and light into yourself. You deserve it.

I am doing everything I can to control and overcome this cunning, baffling disease. I want to accept myself and not feel the compelling urge to be perfect as reflected by my need to be perfectly slender.

At first, I thought if I threw up even one time that meant I was weak. I "should" be able to face anything to really be getting better. But, I also had to face that I needed to build up my repetoire of holding in food so I could get stronger. I guess I had to become easier on me. As I became easier on myself, I became more self-accepting, which enabled me to feel better about myself.

A great decrease in bulimic behavior occured when I got a dog. The dog represented acceptance, companionship, something to love and care for. Gradually, I began to accept and care for myself!

Express Yourself

Improve what you say and how you say it, to yourself and others. Try increasing your use of the pronoun "I," and follow it up with active verbs such as feel, think, want, wish, am! Say "do" instead of "don't!" Stop thinking of yourself as "bulimic," you're "recovering from bulimia." The mind can create problems or solutions, it just depends on what you practice. Replace negative with positive. Rid yourself of belittling thoughts. Keep repeating phrases like, "I love myself," and, "I am worthwhile," until they become your automatic way of thinking. Change your attitude and perspective.

Instead of swallowing your emotions, let them out. Be cheerful! Abandon your fears about talking to people, and be honest in your conversations. Seek out uplifting friends and express your support of each other. Let your family and friends know who you really are. Vow never to lie again. Express your opinion!

Improve your body language to reflect this emerging

pride. Smile more, look happier. Stand up straight. Walk and speak with dignity. Work at it! Scream or punch a boxing bag. Go to a dance or yoga class and leave your inhibitions at home.

Appreciate your sexuality. Have an orgasm! Take a couple of days off for a personal vacation during your menstruation. Consider it a celebration of your womanhood instead of "the curse." I believe that the physical act of gorging and purging is substituted for the act and feelings of sexual intercourse: the slow build-up of intensity, the emotional craving for love, the stroking of the body, the explosion of physical pleasure/pain, and often a conditioned guilt. Bulimia is a way to have predictable physical pleasure alone. Is this true for you?

Take the time to smell the roses! Stop limiting your experiences because of a preoccupation with food. Open your eyes to everything and everyone around you.

Journal Writing

Many people find it difficult to discuss their private thoughts, though it gets easier with practice. One way to start is to write them in a journal. No one else will read what you write, you won't be graded on content or grammar, and you don't have to explain yourself. You can be honest without being afraid. Schedule a block of time everyday for writing, and use your journal during times of stress as well as contemplation. For instance, whenever I had a setback binge, I wrote about it to better understand why I did it. Answer questions, such as "What's wrong with big thighs, and who says so?" Fully answer the questions, going off on tangents. Putting the thoughts down on paper will literally take them off your mind! (We've added more on journal writing, along with writing topics, in "A Two-Week Program to Stop Bingeing.")

Physical Exercise

Moderate exercise was considered helpful by more than 80% of the bulimics surveyed. It provided a release for emotional pressures and was healthy and satisfying. Exercising in an obsessive manner to purge unwanted calories and to attain thinness is not our point here. Although regular, moderate exercise is the best way to lower a person's setpoint, this "diet" concern is totally secondary to ending the binge/purge behavior. Exercise is a tool for recovery, a way to remove yourself from food and feel great at the same time. We do not suggest one form of exercise over another. Team sports are just as helpful as working out by yourself, and you may find that there is more to be gained by being with others. We do, however, stress the importance of stretching before hard exercising. (There is a good short guide to stretching on Day One of "A Two-Week Program to Stop Bingeing.") Here are two endorsements:

I've found exercise helpful. I'll tend to eat normally instead of my usual cram session. I jog, but I suppose any type of exercise that works up a good honest sweat will do.

To help ease the anxiety and frustration, I try to swim or bike ride. This releases a lot of built-up energy that I usually use for a binge (bingeing is exhausting!). After exercising I feel so much better about myself. I'm

*proud because I chose to do something good for me
instead of the same old reliable binge.*

Relax, Relax, Relax!

With few exceptions, people who spend their time
worrying about food have unhealthy stress levels. If
you're always on the move, slow down and learn to
relax. I've heard that watching a bowl of fish for twenty
minutes each day reduces anxiety. Why not, if it
works? You might benefit from listening to music,
quiet walks, staring at a body of water, watching mindless television—anything which rests your mind. I enjoy meditation in particular because I relax, I get time
to myself, and I always feel loving when I am done!
There are many books and tapes available which teach
different techniques. A description of one simple way
to meditate follows, and others are included in the
programs in the appendices. The goal of this activity is
to relax. Do not expect to have mystic hallucinations,
just quiet.

Give yourself at least a fifteen or twenty minute slot
of time. Comfortably sit or lie down in a peaceful spot.
Gently close your eyes, and silently count to ten as you
inhale, again to ten as you hold your breath, and once
more as you exhale. Repeat this three times to slow
down and to focus your mind. Then repeat "I am,"
with each breath, and continue this until the time is
passed. (You may substitute other words, or a mantra,
for "I am," but it is helpful to maintain repetition.) Try
not to be occupied by your thoughts, but allow them to
pass through your mind. This takes practice, and there
are times when your mind may refuse to slow down,
but eventually you will be able to enjoy a state of deep
relaxation.

Spiritual Pursuits

The bulimics who mentioned spirituality as one of their therapies—42% of all the responses described "Spiritual Pursuits" helpful—usually were deeply inspired and motivated, regardless of their faith. The specific religions and practices mentioned were: faith in God, Jesus Christ, or a guru; doing zazen; and embracing Buddhism. Spirituality played a large part in my cure, and remains essential to my daily life. Self-love and love for other people also had a spiritual effect with the same positive consequences for these women:

The main thing that has helped is my faith and trust in God. A lack of security is a problem with eating disorder sufferers and knowing God cares for me, gives me comfort and peace. We all need someone to trust that we know loves us unconditionally, not for how we look or what we do, just for us as we are.

A cure seems to be an impossibility, but practicing self-love instead of self-pity is important. Having faith and confidence in myself also helps. Facing my fears instead of running from them helps, when I do it.

CHAPTER
6

Things to Do Instead of Bingeing

When I felt driven to do a binge, I had a list of activities to turn to. By going to that list instead of the refrigerator, I was able to prevent most binges from occuring. I tried to redirect my time, energy, and money to more productive activities. Do not be reluctant to explore avenues that are outside of your norm. Read this chapter and make your own list. When you are tempted to binge, use those ideas. Here are many suggestions, including some previously mentioned:

* Pamper yourself with a facial, massage, or hot bath. Let yourself feel good, physically.

* Release your anxieties and frustrations with physical activity. Punch a boxing bag or scream into a pillow. I used to wrestle with Leigh, and it felt great to scream and flail around until I was exhausted. I am not suggesting punishing your body, just giving it a royal workout.

* Try to differentiate between your cravings for food and other kinds of cravings. Maybe you are really hungry for love, excitement, or spiritual wholeness.

* Give yourself permission to eat what you crave, but do it with a capable support person who understands your goal is to increase self-awareness, not to binge. Spend time talking about your feelings or writing them down.

* Write in your journal about the feelings and circumstances that are influencing you to binge. Be willing to take as much time as you need. Be intimate and honest, and keep your writings for later reference. Go back and read some of your earliest entries, and see your progress. Try a dream journal, too!

* Call a friend and explain your problem. Support people may not be eager to hear constant complaining, but they will be pleased that they can actually help you not to binge. Cultivate friends who are sensitive, compassionate, and capable of uplifting you. Sometimes it is good to talk to someone who has worked at overcoming an eating disorder.

* Write a letter to a family member about your bulimia. I wrote a few letters to my parents that I never sent, but it still felt good to express myself specifically to them. Eventually, I sent one of the letters and was relieved to tell them the truth.

* Talk to your mother and/or father about your childhood. Get up the courage to ask them about some of those moments of your past that have never been

clear to you. Be prepared for a change in your relationship.

* Contact a childhood friend whom you have thought about but have not seen for some time. Catch up on each others' lives. It will not matter to them that you may have been bulimic for five or ten years. They have their own unique stories to tell.

* Try not to be so perfect. Bulimics are often tidy about every aspect of their lives except their own inner-peace. Don't worry about housework or studying for a while. It is okay not to be perfect about every external matter.

* Pretend to be what you consider "normal" for a day. Make a plan to eat and act like this "normal" person; and, then observe yourself and notice what you do and how it feels.

* Go to a cultural activity (concert, art show, museum, theater, etc.).

* Get involved in volunteer work for a worthwhile cause.

* Learn something new: a foreign language, CPR, a musical instrument, an art medium, some kind of mechanics or electronics, computers, etc. Try out some classes which emphasize self-reliance, assertiveness, or improved body image.

* Concentrate on new ways to make money instead of obsessing about food, and then follow through on

these schemes. As I started to curtail my bingeing, my soft-sculpture business began to grow. Eventually, I found myself thinking more about production than about food. I was rewarded by profits, increased self-esteem, and feelings of independence and self-worth.

* Make lists about your life, things you like and dislike, your goals, and needs. I use lists to complete necessary tasks, arrange my priorities, and get satisfaction by seeing what I have accomplished when I cross things off.

* If you can, stop yourself in the middle of a binge. This may seem impossible, but those who have done it say it is a very powerful accomplishment. Practice saying "NO!" Be assertive and express your needs. It may feel risky, but try it anyway!

Every person who wrote to us had their own unique way of getting better. Many women expressed the hope that their experiences and suggestions would benefit others.

This thirty-four-year-old bulimic of fourteen years improved tremendously in one year after having been anorexic as well as bulimic. She was hospitalized for medical complications, and learned to stop herself from bingeing by using her own, complete approach:

* *Learn to relax and slow down by using exercise, yoga, and meditation.*
* *Enroll in therapy: intensive group in addition to individual.*
* *Practice new behaviors and activities, such as:*

self-improvement classes and hobbies for the early evening hour.

* Change old rules, such as "no eating in the car" and remove the "temptations" of binge food from my house and car.

* Just eat without combining in reading, working, watching tv, etc.

* I talk to myself, "What's the 'pay off' for bingeing this time?"

* Tell myself I would feel worse physically after bingeing and purging.

* Tell myself to "slow down."

* Leave the environment that's tempting me to binge, especially when I'm frustrated, under pressure, stressed or bored.

Here is a comprehensive list of suggestions from our survey:

* I have an easier time if I get enough rest and if I have positive relationships.

* Try to walk away from the food, go somewhere quiet, write down your feelings, or just relax.

* I write down all of my thoughts and then write a rational reply to each argument to binge.

* What helped me once was expressing my feelings in a tape recorder.

* Get your mind on something else. Chew a piece of sugarless gum, turn on the radio and start dancing. Work up a sweat, it's great! Even if you start to jump up

and down and let out a few screams, hit a pillow, it helps get your mind off the binge.

* *Crying helps a lot, too. If I can cry hard for a couple of hours, it relieves me. The next day I wake up feeling happy and not so depressed.*

* *Take deep breaths, close your eyes, picture yourself in a field or at a beach. Turn on quiet music, any method of relaxation helps.*

* *I repeat affirmations daily.*

* *The use of positive language was very helpful. For example, "When I stop bingeing . . . ," and "I may have binged today, but I was bingeing five and six times a day just one month ago."*

* *Tell myself to wait 15 minutes first. Brush my teeth so my mouth tastes clean. Throw away food when I start to binge, or soak it with water.*

* *Sometimes I can just talk myself out of it by convincing myself that I am a nice person and deserve to live happily.*

* *Not starting! Do something else right away before the internal argument begins at all. I will still lose if I try to rationalize with myself.*

* *I get busy with some project immediately after eating a normal meal, since I have trouble quitting after I start eating.*

* *I carry my food rather than buy it at work. I'm*

strong in the morning, so I pack healthy, satisfying food. Otherwise, I'm tempted to eat breads and sweets.

* *I won't binge if I know I can't get rid of it, so if I purposely eat things that are difficult to vomit (oranges, string beans, etc.), I won't binge. Also, going to visit friends will keep me from bingeing and makes me feel better. I reward myself whenever I have the desire and the opportunity to binge, and don't do it.*

* *I call a friend that knows about my problem and have them just listen to me.*

* *A binge is a way I am good to myself, a reward in a strange way, so I sit down and try to decide what other ways I could feel rewarded: lunch with a friend, a new shirt, a new book, take a bubble bath, shop, see a movie, etc. If I don't binge, then I get the reward.*

* *I try to keep busy. I have picked up pleasure reading again, which entails browsing in the library a lot.*

* *I would read, take a walk, brush my hair, play piano, do sit-ups, watch television, clean my room, write in my journal, try on clothes, beat my bed with a tennis racket, chew gum, or take a nap.*

* *Lately, on the days that I work, I don't binge. But on the days I don't work, I keep busy and keep supportive, loving people around, or else you know what happens.*

* *My bulimic behavior greatly decreased when I got*

a dog. She represents unconditional acceptance, companionship, something to love and care for, and a reason to take walks, which provide relaxation, exercise, and an opportunity to get out of the house without having to feel alone.

* *Getting on the scale never made me happy, now I don't weigh myself.*

* *Color analysis really improved my self-image.*

* *One thing that helped a lot was taking a vacation. I was away from my usual routine and even though I ate out in restaurants frequently, I did not have the urge to binge and purge.*

* *I have taken up motorcycle riding.*

* *Keep food locked up with a padlock.*

* *Drawing helps because I don't know enough about it to manipulate it, so it never lies.*

* *I re-evaluate financial priorities and filter binge money into going to movies or buying albums.*

* *Write down ways to create extra money or to offer my services.*

* *I volunteer at a nursing home.*

* *I have become involved in youth work and exercise daily if possible.*

* *I pray "God help me" over and over.*

* *Make memos and signs reading "I Trust Myself."*

* *Visual imagery: Picture yourself mentally going into your kitchen and eating one sandwich, a glass of milk, and a banana, then cleaning up and walking out of the kitchen. It is very effective to see yourself doing something before you do it.*

Getting Past Food Fears

One popular saying I've heard is, "Bulimics should learn to eat to live, instead of live to eat," as though food can be thought of solely as nourishment. Sure, biologically, food is fuel and nothing more; but, to most people it means a lot more. It can provide or deprive us of emotional nourishment as well. We can appreciate food in many ways: its flavor, smell, and texture. It can satisfy, fill, and entertain us. However, it is for many a way to abuse, be judgmental, be habitual, feel guilty, and afraid. Every individual with bulimia has myths and rules about eating and food. Some are obvious: "I'm supposed to eat all the food on my plate." Others are more subtle, "If I don't eat all the food on my plate, my mother will be mad." Many of these associations can be recognized and eliminated, especially if they are tackled head on in a systematic and determined manner. Objectivity helps!

At one point in my cure, I was allowing myself a little bit of forbidden foods and lost "control" with a binge. Afterwards, when I reflected on it, I realized I had been afraid to eat and eat and keep eating without throwing up. I decided to confront that "food fear" by doing an all-day binge, without throwing up. Leigh agreed to do it with me for support and fun! Together, we ate "junk" food all day. It was the largest binge I had ever done without vomiting. I accepted the painfully bloated stomach, because I was so happy! I felt expanded, bigger, and instead of embarrassment and fear, this bigness filled me with a sense of accomplishment and power. I had faced my issue and lived to tell about it! (While I do recommend this activity as a step towards curing bulimia, I strongly advise that you do it ONLY WITH PROPER SUPPORT. Under no circumstances attempt anything so extreme by yourself.)

Do not belittle this challenge! For all the insight into the "whys" of your bulimia, the fact remains that YOU WANT TO EAT WITHOUT VOMITING. Some situations will be harder to handle than others. You may even have setback binges. At those times, remember that you are going through a process. Practice patience and self-love. A good way to become more relaxed about what you eat is to experiment with (even a taste of) different foods and cuisines. Try "gentle eating" and appreciating what you eat, instead of gobbling down your meals in a mindless trance. Try cooking with reverence or serving with style! Does this sound like an advertisement? I'm trying to sell you on eating and enjoying it!

Some women from our survey regimented their meals, while others loosened up. Several women mentioned that they learned how to eat by watching other people. One thirty-nine-year-old woman who recovered after twenty-five years of bulimia developed a daily "eating form," which included a listing of all foods eaten, where, with whom, how much, and the calories. There were also boxes to be checked for water, room for affirmations, space to list exercise, supplements, and notes. Here are some other tactics:

I don't eat as normally as I'd like to. I still can't go out for pizza and ice cream with the gang and feel comfortable. However, I have now been trying to eat three meals a day. When I eat a good meal, I try to visualize all of the nutrients rushing through my abused body and revitalizing my whole self. It makes me feel better to know that my body is getting something good for a change, instead of sugar-laden binge foods.

I became willing to be stuffed without vomiting. Now I work on not stuffing myself.

I listen to my body needs which have become clearer now that I am no longer bingeing. I do not follow a rigid food plan.

I really needed to be taught how to eat again. I wanted someone to plan my meals. I started on the right track by following the Weight Watcher's program because I felt it was nutritionally sound. I told myself that there will always be cheesecake or chocolate, bread, whatever! If I don't eat it now it won't be gone forever.

I've been on a diet since I was a chunky ten-year-old. Learning to eat "normally" is the hardest part. I've known no other style of eating other than bingeing and dieting. I still catch myself counting calories and judging myself. It's still hard to decipher my body signals. I feel it is essential that I do not ban any food items from my diet. If I restrict sugar, I crave it and binge on it. I try to eat only when I am hungry and not bored or tired.

A thirty-four-year-old recovering bulimic who has tried several therapy options with marked progress commented:

Don't be fooled into thinking there won't be a flare-up from time to time. I allow myself to mess up without the guilt though. It took time to acquire this technique. If I feel a real need for a binge when the pressure is on or I feel anxious about something, I go ahead and allow it to happen. I try to search out my feelings of anxiety to uncover the problem, and in most cases this prevents or shortens a binge.

I allow myself anything I want, BUT IN MODERA- TION. I have cake and ice cream, bread and butter, even cream in my coffee. The serving size is just small. Being able to allow myself anything to eat has taken away the guilt where before one bite of a "forbidden food" would lead to a binge. I eat it, enjoy it, and keep it down.

There are no forbidden foods for me. Certain foods don't have the power over me that I once gave them.

I try to eat nutritious foods that I know my body needs in an amount that won't make me fat. If I do eat an unallowed, empty-calorie junk food, then I have prob- lems. There are certain foods that I know will trigger a binge, so I have to stay away from them entirely. Car- rots or popcorn satisfy my "munchie" cravings and fruit my sweet cravings. I try not to buy the things I know I'll have trouble with.

I am learning to eat when I'm hungry and not to eat when I'm not hungry. If possible, I try to eat several

*times a day in small portions. The foods that I eat now
leave me feeling satisfied and I have no desire to binge.
Once in a while, I may binge, but the binges are
smaller than they used to be.*

*Allowing myself all foods in small quantities has
helped me, although I must remind myself I "deserve"
cakes, cookies, etc. Cutting out all sugars set me up to
binge, which reinforced that I was "bad" and couldn't
control myself. I pretended not to eat sugar and carbohydrates, only to binge on them in private. I now eat
sweets in small amounts in front of everyone, not trying to be "perfect" in my diet.*

C H A P T E R
8

Encouragement

The most important thing that I can say about the struggle to end bulimia is that it is definitely worth it! That was hard to believe in the early days of my recovery when life seemed to get worse instead of better. I was used to being serious, anxious, and unhappy. I knew my friends had high opinions of me, but only because I kept the "dark me" hidden. Ending my bulimia meant giving up this secret side.

So, I practiced having a new identity, one with no secrets. I tried being cheerful, brave, and open to people. I repeated affirmations, looked for solutions, and accepted help. I dared to feel light, happy and free. I tried reacting to old hurts in new ways, and began to have courage and trust myself. These days, there are no bulimic thoughts left to replace. I am happy, and my life is a reflection of this.

Inside of you is a marvelous, worthwhile, loving, beautiful person. In your heart, you know this is true! Free that self, because that is who you really are! Stick to your commitment, continue to do things instead of bingeing, re-define your concepts, and believe in yourself. Make lists, get support, enter therapy, follow our two-week program. It takes time for such a big change. Don't worry! Be willing to do anything to get better. You can do it! Perhaps the genuine happiness that is expressed by the following quotes will encourage you in your recovery:

I've found a new self-image, more self-esteem, and have learned coping skills through therapy. I've been bulimic for twelve years; and, in a little less than three months, I'm quickly recovering.

I'm highly motivated, as most bulimics are, so treatment has been fast and effective. Group has been very good for me in dealing with family problems. It's good to see how others have made progress, and how they handle their slips.

Every aspect of my life has changed. I have tremendous value and self-worth. I am very productive, confident, enjoy beautiful relationships with family and friends, enjoy intimacy to the max, enjoy my children, am going through a divorce, and am happy about that, too!

I still binge and find it difficult to stop, but they are not nearly as large as they once were. I remind myself that no food will satisfy my emotions of loneliness or nervousness. I also try to let the emotion that sets up the binge happen, and relax.

Most of the time I'm fairly serene and better able to cope now that I'm no longer escaping through food. It's also more painful though, because I must deal with the emotions instead of covering them up.

The weeks I have been completely free of bulimia, I sleep better, have more energy, am less nervous, happier, I laugh more, and I'm told I'm more outgoing and fun to be with. I also have more money and more time to do the things I really enjoy.

I feel much more grown up, and that is wonderful. I am more confident. I don't avoid walking into a room of people. I approach each task with more strength. I enjoy little things. I am not so self-centered.

I feel 100% better, am thinner and look much better. I enjoy things, and there's great pride in knowing I've recovered, which gives me added self-confidence about myself.

Physically I feel great. My hair is better, I just look and feel more attractive. I take better care of myself. I love my husband more. I am going back to college and I feel a lot happier and much more relaxed.

I have unending energy. I no longer have terrible cramps in my feet at night, and I'm more mentally alert. The fog has lifted. My hands and feet no longer tingle.

I trust myself more. I know I can enjoy myself when I go out, because my evening won't be disrupted by lengthy trips to the bathroom. I am no longer in a trap, living in a world of "if onlys." Life is much better since I've stopped, I don't feel like such a freak.

Since I'm no longer in the throws of bulimia, I'm feeling more ups and downs and learning how to ex-

press what I'm feeling. I no longer anesthetize myself with food.

I now eat a well-balanced diet, avoiding sweets, caffeine, and alcohol; and, I eat three meals a day. I exercise from forty-five minutes to one hour daily. My confidence has increased, as well as my self-respect. I am rarely depressed any more, and find enjoyment in life again. I have a choice now.

Suddenly, I have the time to get my work all done and play, too. I have much more money for hobbies. Believe me, alcoholics only have about one-tenth the financial problems that bulimics do. I could eat up $150 a day, enough for a fair-sized coke habit, I'd say! I'm settled now, happy, and eager for tomorrow.

Seventeen years is a long time to be in prison. I've done my time. I've earned my freedom. For me there are no concrete events or even attitudes in my cure rather an existential decision in favor of life which I continually affirm.

I can't believe in reviewing this list [the "progress" question in the survey] that I overcame all of these problems! After 20 years of bulimia, it took me two years of gradual improvement. It was difficult indeed and I have a very good feeling about myself for making it!

A Two-Week Program to Stop Bingeing

The purpose of this section is to give bulimics specific goals and tasks to help them stop bingeing. It's an instant support group! It can also provide insights into the recovery process for those readers who are interested.

Read through the entire agenda to get an idea of what the assignments will be. Even if you are not ready to start the course, you can benefit from trying some of the techniques without following the daily routine. We recommend the same things that we talk about in this book: journal writing, relaxation, moderate exercise, professional therapy, talking to people, etc. Once you've read the program through, you'll have lots of thoughts and inspiration to stop bingeing.

The course requires spending time and effort. You will practice having fun, being loving, thinking happy thoughts, and getting to know yourself. These can be a habit, too! If you use this plan faithfully, you may not binge for two weeks; and, you will have more skills and confidence to help you to stop bingeing for good. If you do binge, you have not failed. You are given criteria to understand what has happened and guidelines to prevent the next binge. Whether you stop your bulimia is up to you, during the two weeks, and afterwards. We are providing only a framework for your recovery. We'll hold your hand by supporting you with our suggestions and our "presence," but you must do the work.

Let us remind you again that your bulimia has served you in many ways, most notably to protect you from painful feelings. Experiencing past hurts, present shame, or any other unfamiliar, unexpressed feelings can be frightening and overwhelming. Be aware that these feelings are varied and extremely powerful. Moreover, if you are not used to experiencing feelings or even differentiating one from another, you may be tempted to turn to your familiar friend bulimia for safety. Can you understand how natural this is? Can you have compassion for yourself given the task ahead of you?

Our advice is to be aware and be prepared. If you are not yet in therapy, have someone or something to support you—a friend, relative, hotline, cassette tapes of your own soothing voice or special music, books on feelings, or a notebook. Now might be a good time for you to start.

D A Y   1

My life is better without bulimia!

Hooray! You are making a commitment to end your bulimia, and you'll be happy that you did! Since this is your first day, we will have orientation. In the future, the instructions will not include as many details. If Day

1 begins in the afternoon, do everything anyway; but, tomorrow, you will need to start at the beginning of the day. Be prepared to spend some money for materials and field trips. These costs are generally low, and by the end of the course you will have saved money that you probably would have spent on food. TODAY, buy a three-ring notebook, five dividers, and paper specifically for this course. Keep it and *Eating Without Fear* next to your bed, and as soon as you get up in the morning, turn to the appropriate page and get started.

First Things First: Every day, as soon as you can, but definitely before eating, you have a few things to do (in order): Read the Thought for the Day, do the Morning Warmup, read the entire day's plan in this book, and work in your notebook.

IMPORTANT NOTE: This program offers you the experience of freedom from bulimia. This is *not* a test. There is no right or wrong way to do it. Stick to it faithfully or choose activities and give them a try.

Thought for the Day: My life is better without bulimia!

Keep repeating this thought over and over all day. Say it to yourself when you sit down and when you stand up, when you open doors, while driving, while washing your hands, twice when you eat, etc. Every day you will be given another thought. Say it with conviction and belief, and most of all, repeat it!

The Morning Warmup: If you have to go to the bathroom, you may. If you have roommates, husbands, kids, or others that require your attention, make them wait, participate, or support you in any way necessary to afford you this short bit of time.

Today, let's start with a good stretch. It will take about ten minutes. Put on some music, if you wish.

Here are some hints for getting the most from stretching:

1. Instead of copying someone else's routine, make up your own as you go along. Unlearn rules about keeping joints straight or repetitions.

2. Don't bounce or try to be flexible. Relax and enjoy feeling your muscles. Touch them with your fingers.

3. Groan, sigh, laugh, and breathe noisily—it's fun and releases tension.

4. Slowly, stretch your whole body.

5. If you feel tension in your face, there is tension in your body—relax your face!

6. Don't overstretch. If it starts to hurt, then relax, breathe, and don't push yourself to go further than you can. Stretching should feel good!

7. Give yourself about ten minutes. Include your: eyes, neck, back, shoulders, chest, arms, fingers, thighs, calves, and feet. Alternate bending and arching your back, twisting one direction and then the other, etc. Also, remember to keep repeating the Thought for the Day.

Your Notebook

Every day there will be assignments of things to write about, places to go, or exercises to do. Do them any time, before or after meals, instead of bingeing, whenever you can. We strongly suggest that you do all of the assignments, but there may be times when you cannot. Do each day's work that day, and if necessary, catch up afterwards.

Arrange your notebook with five dividers labeled: Journal, Options, Binge, Written Homework, and Other. Today, we will explain about each section:

Journal: Sometimes you will be given journal writing assignments, but you should also use this space whenever you have something to say. Always copy the Thought for the Day into your journal.

Options: Every day we will provide a few suggestions for things you can do instead of bingeing. You should also write some of your own ideas. Emphasize techniques that work. One requirement of this course is that you consult this list if you are on the verge of a binge.

Today's Options:

1. Punch, kick, yell, and go wild! Use an appropriate object, such as beds and pillows, boxing bags, or willing friends. We used to fight with boxing gloves and wrestle. Vent your frustrations and tensions, and loudly express those feelings which you've been swallowing. Look at a clock and go five rounds of two minutes each. Make that pillow feel your anger, beat the #$%!! out of it!

2. Get away, quick! Go to a quiet restful place where food is not easily available, such as a park, beach, museum, church, or library. Bring your notebook and write in your journal. Use the relaxation or meditation techniques described in the "What Has Worked For Many" section of this book.

3. Work on today's homework.

4. Exercise! Be sure to stretch first, and pace yourself—don't over-exert. If you have a favorite way of

exercising, do that. Otherwise, lightly jog and walk for an hour, or take a long bicycle ride. Isn't that about how long you might spend on a binge?

5. Make a list of three options of your own, and do one of those.

Binge: Reward yourself with a sheet in this section when you resist the temptations to binge. You might describe how you felt not bingeing, what options worked for you, or glue in a photo that expresses your feelings, or words of wisdom that may have inspired or entertained you that day.

What if you do binge? Don't give up! Would you quit school if you received a poor grade on one assignment? No, you would realize that more study is necessary. HERE IS YOUR EXTRA HOMEWORK IF YOU HAVE BINGED:

1. Write about the binge. You may include answers to some of these questions: What led you to do the binge? What were your thoughts before and during? What did you eat? Did you purge, how? What were you feeling? Did you try to do something instead of bingeing? Why didn't that work? What else could you have done? What will you try to do instead of bingeing next time the cravings are so strong?

2. Glue in a photo that reminds you of the binge. Some ideas: cut out a magazine advertisement for junk food and put a big black X over it, write over a diet advertisement with the words "Weight is not important to me, loving myself is!" or, a news clipping that reminds you that you are still better off than some unfortunate people.

3. Spend ten minutes relaxing. See Today's Option #2.

Written Homework: This notebook section will be or keeping your written assignments.

Other: This section is for any additional writing, lippings, souvenirs, etc. Be sure to stock your note-ook with plenty of paper and attach a couple of extra ens or pencils to the inside cover so they will always e handy. It's a good idea to carry a notepad wherever ou go, just in case you have an inspiring idea to ecord.

Homework: Day 1

1. Write about your bingeing habits of the last week, 1onth, and years. Include frequency of binges and urges, and describe in detail your last binge. You will efer to this assignment later during the course, so be ure to leave it in the "Written Homework" section.

2. Write a final journal entry before going to sleep onight. Include what you did today, how you felt, and ome reflections on this course. Be sure to write, "My fe is better without bulimia!" Life really is better vithout it.

Good Night: If today was hard for you, stick to it, ecause as the days progress, the program will help ou stop bingeing. Even if we haven't met personally, ve want you to know that we love you and completely upport your efforts. We encourage you to write us bout your experiences, and we will write back! Re-nember to read Day 2 as soon as you wake up, but rest vith the knowledge that you are worthwhile, strong, nd you're going to make it! Sleep well.

D A Y   2

Look for solutions, not problems

Good morning! We hope you slept well. If you ar
excited about this course to end your bulimia, grea
Let's get started.

First Things First: Read the Thought for the Day, do th
Morning Warmup, read the entire day's plan, and the
write a short journal entry (see below).

Thought for the Day: Look for solutions, not problem
It's your mind that creates problems. It can creat
anything, abundance or scarcity, happiness or worr
Notice your belittling thoughts and get rid of them
You are not unworthy, you just think that you ar
Today, look on the bright side; in other words, look fo
solutions, not problems!

The Morning Warmup: Take a long, hot shower o
bath. By all means, sing at least one song out loud
Gently stretch and massage yourself as you bathe
Think about what we've planned for you to do today
what you will write about in your journal, and what wi
be acceptable for you to eat for breakfast.

Short Journal Entry: Describe one of the happiest mo
ments of your life. Try to remember why you felt s
good about yourself then. We want you to remin
yourself of that good feeling throughout the day.

Today's Options:

1. Gather your binge food and soak it with water in the sink. Don't concern yourself with the waste, you would have wasted it by bingeing.

2. Take another shower or bath, repeat everything that you did in the Morning Warmup.

3. Drink water or eat a carrot.

4. Tell yourself to slow down, relax. Spend fifteen to thirty minutes in deep relaxation or meditation.

5. Review yesterday's options and your own list. Choose something that will work!

6. Work on Today's Assignments.

Homework: Day 2

1. Write answers to these questions: What are your bulimia goals for these two weeks? For after the course? What are your goals for today? What kind of meals do you want to eat? How much food would make you feel good about yourself? What do you want to do immediately after breakfast?

2. Begin compiling your SUPPORT LIST. Make one list of all the people who already know about your bulimia. Make another list of everyone you will tell. This list should include practically everyone who is close to you. You will not be contacting these people yet, so there will be some time to get used to this idea.

Now, make a loose order of those you will contact first, second, etc. Include the people who already know, because by contacting them you are seeking their support in helping you to work on your recovery. Let them know that you are really serious about getting better! Write or talk to someone whom you expect to be understanding and supportive first. Next to their names, indicate the probable method of contact that you will use, such as: phone calls, letters, in-person, etc. Getting support is one way of looking for solutions.

3. Today, begin thinking about something new you want to learn. This learning will not have to end at the completion of these two weeks. Some ideas: yoga, a musical instrument, a foreign language, figure drawing, CPR, skydiving, etc. You will be required to spend some time on this, so it should be a fun activity for you.

4. Go for a one hour walk in your neighborhood. Weather is no obstacle, a brisk walk in the rain or snow can be invigorating. Bring your notepad to record any ideas that you have during the walk. Stop to smell the roses! Smile and talk to people you see, look them in the eye. Observe everything, even the sky. Do not eat or go into any stores during this walk.

IMPORTANT NOTE: We often recommend that you get away; but, when you return it is equally important to carry on the feelings that kept you from bingeing. As soon as you return home, sit quietly for five minutes and relax. After that, write in your journal. Other options are to call someone, drink a cup of hot tea, take a shower or bath, or do whatever else works for you. As helpful as it is to get away, it is crucial to maintain your positive feelings and actions upon return.

Good night: You may be experiencing some joy and accomplishment, you may be frustrated and anxious. Regardless of how it went, another day has passed. Reaffirm to yourself that you will continue this course of recovery. You can do it! You are doing it! As you drift off to sleep tonight, remember that moment of happiness we asked you to write about earlier. Put yourself in that situation, feel the warmth and love. Somewhere nearby, we are there, too, thinking of you as a wonderful, loving person. Sweet dreams!

D A Y 3

Lighten up!

Today is going to be a fun day. Too often, people with eating disorders are serious. Everyone has a sense of humor, but sometimes life's pressures prevent us from having a good laugh. Today, laugh! It feels great! Rearrange your schedule if necessary to get the most enjoyment out of today's assignments.

First Things First: Read the Thought for the Day, do the Morning Warmup, read the entire day's plan in this book, and review the options in your notebook.

Thought for the Day: Lighten up! (This has nothing to do with your weight!)

The Morning Warmup: Bring a watch or clock into the bathroom with you and lock the door. Spend no less than five minutes looking at your face in the mirror. The longer, the better. Try not to look away. Make extended eye contact with yourself. Who is that? When is the last time you really looked at your face? Look at all of the colors in your eyes, did you ever notice that before? When you look at someone else, what do you base your judgments on? What kinds of judgments do you make about yourself? How about making some new, positive affirmations about yourself?

Make dopey faces in the mirror. Stretch your face, wiggle your lips, squish your nose, pull on your ears, etc. Grunt, squeak, say "Ho ho ho," "ha ha ha," and "he he he." Laugh out loud, even if it's a phony laugh. Come on, lighten up, really get silly!

While you're in the bathroom, talk out loud to your scale. (See Today's Homework #5.) Tell it that you resent its influence over you. Have a good heart-to-heart with it!

Today's Options:

1. Write affirmations in your journal 50 times, such as: "I trust myself," "I won't binge today," or "Every day in every way I'm getting better and better." As long as you are still tempted to binge, keep writing!

2. Go for a walk.

3. Do one of today's assignments, there's a lot to do today.

4. Review what has worked and been suggested before.

Homework: Day 3

1. Go to a bookstore today to do these first two homework assignments. Look for books that will help you start your new learning project, which was mentioned in yesterday's homework. Buy one if you're ready.

2. At the bookstore, read through joke books. Laugh out loud right there in the bookstore, even a phony laugh is acceptable! Also, look through Norman Cousin's writings. Spend no time in the "diet" or "cooking" sections unless they are part of your study project. If you're really ambitious, also go to a record or video store and buy or rent a comedy recording.

3. Contact someone from your support list to tell some of the new jokes that you read today. This conversation isn't necessarily the time to talk about your bulimia, but that would be okay, too.

4. Write a letter to the first "letter" person on your support list. You do not have to send it.

5. If you weigh yourself a lot on a home scale, it has to stop. If you can, destroy it! One woman threw hers from the 34th floor of a high-rise apartment building into a swimming pool below which had been emptied for winter. A hammer will work just fine, though running over it with a car may be equally satisfying. Don't just throw it away, destroy it and laugh.

Good night: We hope that this day has been as enjoyable for you as it has been for us. We got a couple of good giggles from the plan, did you?

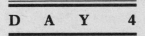

D A Y 4

I can eat without fear!

You may have noticed that we haven't said much about food or eating yet. Today, we will! Whatever the cause of your bulimia—whether it be family, society, chemical imbalance, karma, a desire to be thin, or anything else—you still need to eat. Don't wait to understand all your "whys" because that in itself will not stop you from bingeing. Appreciate food for its taste and nourishment, and let go of your negative, obsessive thoughts.

First Things First: Read the Thought for the Day, do the Morning Warmup, read the entire day's plan in this book, and do the short journal entry which is assigned.

Thought for the Day: I can eat without fear.

The Morning Warmup: Do a short, five minute stretch. If you need to refresh your memory about stretching, re-read the guidelines from Day 1.

Morning Journal Entry: Plan today's menu. Include breakfast, lunch, dinner, snacks, and a small, acceptable dessert. Be specific, you will go shopping for groceries later. Your meals today should be balanced, tasty, and non-threatening. Stick to this menu faithfully.

Today's Options:

1. Buy a plant or new pet, such as a goldfish or turtle.

2. Call someone from your support list.

3. Work on your new study project or today's assignments.

4. Ask yourself: What's the payoff to bingeing? How does that compare with the satisfaction of not bingeing? Then, just don't do it!

5. As always, review the other days' options.

Homework: Day 4

1. Take the first few names from the support list you compiled on Day 2. If you plan on talking to them, draft some of the sentences first. Include questions that you want to ask, and specific things that you want them to do for you. It is important to have a support person to call when you are craving a binge. For more ideas, consult "Specific Advice for Loved Ones."

2. You need to go grocery shopping. Make a detailed list and buy only the food you need for the menu that you have prepared. Do not buy anything that is not on your list. Stick to your menu. You can do it!

3. Bring your notepad to the grocery. Write down the name and price of every item of food that you would eat on a binge. In your notebook, copy this list and write down the total of how much you would have spent. Then take the original list and either burn it, tear it up, or eat it!

4. Have a special meal today. Eat by candlelight, with soft music, or with the good china. Practice gentle eating. Put your utensil down between bites, taste your food, savor each bite.

5. Re-read the chapter in this book, "Getting Past Food Fears."

Good night: Many people say that food is not the issue for bulimics; and, while we agree with this in principal, we still emphasize that reformed eating habits are crucial for recovery. The binge-purge behavior was learned, now it must be unlearned. Let your friends help you, and believe in yourself. Stick to this program! Even if we've never met you, we care about you, we really do.

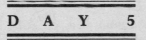

D A Y   5

Think lovely thoughts!

Have you been earnestly following the guidelines of the past four days? Have you done the Morning Warm-ups everyday, repeated the Thought for the Day, written in your journal, and worked on the assignments? How many support people have you talked to about your bulimia? Have you started studying something new? Have you binged, or have you tried the no-binge options?

The suggestions that we make day-to-day requi
you to work all day, not just for a few moments whi
you read the page or do an assignment. The actu
assignments are secondary to the effort that you p
into them. You are setting the goals and followir
through to achieve them. Think about them as you ea
rest, bathe, walk, talk, etc. When faced with pressu
and temptation, be strong and fight. Beat the feathe
out of that pillow, soak the binge food, get away, see
help from those who truly do love you. You are wort
while and would help them if they needed it. Now yc
need help, ask for it and accept it.

First Things First: Read the Thought for the Day, do th
Morning Warmup, read the entire day's plan in th
book, and write in your journal.

Thought for the Day: See the positive, in everyone ar
everything. If you begin to have a negative though
stop and replace it with a positive one. Conscious
and actively practice feelings of love, approval, ar
goodness.

The Morning Warmup: See yourself a little differentl
Spend about twenty minutes doing this relaxation exe
cise: In a quiet place, lie flat on your back, eyes close
You will tense and then relax every part of your bod
Start with your toes and feet, flexing them, holding th
tension, and then releasing, allowing that area to gentl
relax. Slowly follow this procedure up your calve
knees, thighs, buttocks, genitals, waist, chest, bacl
shoulders, arms, etc. By the time you have rested you
entire body, spend a few minutes carefully observir
each of these visions: See yourself in a mirror, look a
yourself without judgment. Then metamorphose you

image into other shapes and forms, such as: tremendously fat, skinny, tall, as a midget, as several different races, as the opposite sex, and as pure light without form.

You may fall asleep during this exercise, so as a precaution you might want to set an alarm.

Morning Journal Entry: Write one sentence each about five to ten good things in your life.

Today's Options:

1. Look at how much money you saved yesterday by not buying binge food. Think of an enjoyable way to use that amount of money, then go ahead and spend!

2. Work with diligence on your study project.

3. Review past options.

Homework: Day 5

1. Write a physical description of yourself. Include what you saw in the mirror yesterday when you studied your face, your hands, skin complexion and texture, hair, legs, etc. Who do you look like? What are some judgments you've made about your body? Do you wish that there were differences? What are they? Are they reasonable or even possible?

2. Buy a magazine with a large, women's mass market. When you get home, go through the ads, articles, and photos. Tear out everything that appeals to or depicts thin women, food, diets, or beautifying products, such as cosmetics. How much of the magazine is left? Why is the torn out pile so large? Reflect on the economics and message of the medium in your journal.

Tear the junk pile to shreds, while you repeat today's Thought for the Day.

3. Whenever you have a negative thought today, write it down, then tear up the paper. Replace the thought with a positive one!

4. IMPORTANT: Review the plan for Day 9, you will be going on an all-day excursion. You may have to do some rearranging of your schedule and planning ahead, so start today. You might want to contact a friend to accompany you.

5. Allow yourself a small dessert tonight. Do not obsess about it, merely select and eat your sweet tonight as a reward for your efforts to end your bulimia. Do not count calories. If you begin to even think negative thoughts after eating your dessert, immediately stop what you are doing and write your thoughts in your journal. After that entry, spend ten or fifteen minutes stretching or going for a walk.

Good night: Words, whether spoken or thought, have tremendous power. The way that we verbalize something is how we perceive of it. If negative words are used, negative feelings surface. Any event can be thought of in many different ways. Rarely will two people have an identical impression of the same event. You may have gotten used to thinking of yourself as bulimic, worthless, unlovable, or unattractive. You must change those thoughts. Think of yourself as recovering from bulimia, worthy, lovable, and attractive.

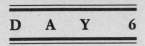

D A Y 6

I can accept support from others

We hope you had sweet dreams from your lovely thoughts of yesterday. Keep practicing and looking on the bright side. Goodness is attracted to cheerful people, and their radiance is obvious.

First Things First: Read the Thought for the Day, do the Morning Warmup, read the entire day's plan in this book, and work in your notebook.

Thought for the Day: I can accept support from others.
   Getting support does not mean having horribly serious talks. A support relationship can be fun for both people. By asking someone to help you stop bingeing and purging, you are being honest, respecting that person's point-of-view, and deepening the bonds of friendship. What could be better than that? You have many new experiences from this program alone, share them!

The Morning Warmup: Loosen up with a quick, five minute stretch, followed by a long, hot shower. If you have any body oil, splash it on!

Today's Options:

1. Talk to a neighbor. Even casual conversation can distract you from bingeing.
2. Pamper your pets or plants.
3. Consult your own list and pick one of the first three ideas.

Homework: Day 6

1. Review your support list and pick one local person. Tell them that you have something important to talk about tonight, and also ask them to go with you to a movie. Television is okay as a second choice. Meet at least an hour or two before the show starts to have enough time to talk about your bulimia. Follow that with some good clean fun! If you have a previous commitment that cannot be broken, schedule this for the first available night. Make plans now!

2. (You may already be doing this one.) Begin to arrange for at least one session of professional therapy. Re-read the answers to "How should I choose a therapist?" in the "Questions Most Often Asked About Bulimia" section and the Professional Therapy section. At the very least, make a list of therapists.

3. Confront your feelings about family members. Choose one member of your family, and then write about how they have affected you in the following way (we'll use Mom as an example, you may pick anyone). During your lifetime what specific thing has Mom said or done that you have held on to? How did you feel? How did you react? Why has this event stuck with you? What do you wish you had said or done at the time? What could she have said or done to convey her message in a more positive manner? Could the two of you have talked? Is it worth talking about now?

4. Continue writing about your family and how they can support you. Answer these questions: How do they support you now? Are they doing their best? What can you do to improve your relationship with your family? Can you accept their love?

5. (optional) Talk to a family member about your bulimia recovery.

Good night: Was the movie good? Was it as entertaining as your conversation with your support person? We bet that you are a pretty likable person after all! Of the hundreds of people who have confessed their bulimia to us—we are sometimes the first ones told—each one has been sensitive, pleasant, and usually able to joke. Great qualities!

D A Y 7

Peace of Mind

Today you will be half-way through this program to stop bingeing. Think about it for a moment. Have your binges decreased this week? Most of the course emphasis so far has been on getting to know yourself better. Next week, we will encourage you to interact more. Today, you deserve to take it a little easier; but, that does not mean to slack off on your commitment to doing the homework and not bingeing.

First Things First: Read the Thought for the Day, do the Morning Warmup, read the entire day's plan in this book, and work in your notebook.

Thought for the Day: I deserve rest and relaxation.
Many bulimics are high-achievers and feel guilty if they are not being productive. Life is not a race or contest, and everyone needs to kick back at times. If bingeing has been a way for you to unwind or be entertained, you need new outlets.

The Morning Warmup: Use the progressive relaxation technique from Day 5 up to the part about looking in a mirror. Today, when you are in that state of deep physical relaxation, visualize a special place. This can be somewhere that you know well, or it can be imagined. Put yourself there by seeing everything, hearing the sounds of that place, smelling the air, and feeling your entire being in that restful scene.

Today's Options:

1. Chew gum, a carrot, or a celery stick.
2. Flush your binge food down the toilet before you eat it.
3. Repeat this morning's relaxation and return to your special place.
4. Review options that have worked before.

Homework: Day 7

1. Write or call someone you love. We recommend seeking out a person whom you have not seen for a long time, but care for, such as a childhood friend or lost relative.
2. Read the plan for Day 9, and make any necessary preparations.
3. Rest your mind by watching at least one hour of television. We watch soap operas! Television can have a tranquilizing effect.
4. (optional) Work on your study project.
5. Today, avoid speaking whenever possible. Try to reflect more on your inner-thoughts. Silence is wonderful!

Good night: We suggest that you get to bed early tonight, and enjoy a long sleep. Congratulations on sticking to the program for a week, it's all downhill from here!

D A Y   8

Love Day!

Today is "Love Day" and you're going to love it! Last week we concentrated on inner-growth. This week we are going to expand our horizons to include more people, places, and outside experiences.

First Things First: Read the Thought for the Day, do the Morning Warmup, read the entire day's plan in this book, and write in your journal.

Thought for the Day: I love everyone and everything, unconditionally and completely. Love doesn't come from "out there." If you think no one loves you, that your parents didn't, your friends don't, and you're sure that the "right" guy or gal won't, how then, can you love yourself? You must become the source of love. Create love, feel comfortable. Trust that you are loved by yourself and by others. Practice this trust.

The Morning Warmup: Take a sensual shower or hot bath. Don't just soak or wash, but massage your muscles. Appreciate the sensuality of your skin. Touch yourself with a lover's embrace. If your situation permits, share this experience.

Short Journal Entry: What is your definition of "love"?

Today's Options:

1. Let's review a few from last week: exercise, soak food, beat up a pillow, get away, drink water, read your joke book. Have you tried these yet?

2. Take a round-trip bus ride anywhere. Observe the people on the bus, practice seeing each of them through loving eyes. Do not eat on this trip!

3. Try prayer.

4. Get a professional massage or facial.

Homework: Day 8

1. Do a good deed. Some possibilities: go to a nursing home and volunteer your time talking to an elderly person, babysit for a friend with small children, visit someone and help them clean or cook, go to a non-profit organization and offer your services, etc. Don't just call or think about it. This is the main assignment today, go somewhere and do it!

2. Tell someone you love them.

3. Continue work on these earlier assignments: arranging for professional therapy, and contacting people from your support list.

4. Have you lined up someone to join you on Day 9?

5. Throughout the day, look at your reflection in different mirrors and windows. Think about it. Does your mood depend on what you see?

6. (optional) Go to a bookstore and get a book on "Love" or "Loving," such as those by Leo Buscaglia.

Good night: Everyday can be a "Love Day" if you practice. Love is not something that comes from outside of yourself. As we wrote this book, feelings of love generated the words. Doing good deeds, helping others, feeling good about ourselves, these give us a purpose for living.

D A Y 9

It's all right to be different

Invite someone to join you in today's role playing. Today's work should be fun and revealing. We become so caught up in our identities, and our own particular roles. We act in ways to please our parents, bosses, teachers, and friends. What about you? Do you live for others with little regard for your own feelings? Do you want to be thin to please a lover, parent, or society? Who makes judgments about you? Is it okay to be different from the norm? Don't be afraid of what people will think, be fearless!

First Things First: Today, read the entire day's plan first. Then, read the Thought for the Day, do the Morning Warmup, and write in your journal.

Thought for the Day: It's all right to be different. Today, you will be! Create a new identity for yourself and act it out! Of course, you must choose not to be bulimic. It doesn't have to be someone exotic, it might be what you consider to be a "normal" person.

The Morning Warmup: As you know by reading today's plan, you are going to pretend to be someone else today. Wash your hair and fix it a way that this other person would wear it, maybe with scarf, curls, parted in the middle, etc. Get dressed as this person would dress. If you usually wear pants, maybe you'll wear a dress, and high heels. If you usually wear makeup, maybe this person won't. As you "put on your costume" begin to assume the new identity.

Morning Journal Entry: Write about the person you are pretending to be today. What's your name? What are your likes and dislikes? What's your background? What special talents do you have? What do you like to eat? Make your description interesting, and complete. Then become that person for the day.

Today's Options:

1. The person you're pretending to be doesn't binge!
2. Use your support person.
3. Do what has worked before.

Homework: Day 9

1. Today you will be going on an all day excursion. If it is absolutely impossible for you to call-in sick at work or play hooky from school, then substitute this day for the earliest one possible.

2. You've been instructed to read today's lesson and to get a friend to join you today. Warn your friend in advance that you are going to be "in character" and he or she should, too. It may sound crazy and you might be slightly embarrassed to suggest it, but it will be fun for both of you.

Obviously, it will be difficult to continue this mascarade all day. Don't worry about it. Be that person as much as possible, and use this distance to get to know yourself better.

3. Go away all day. Get far away from your usual surroundings, preferably to a beautiful, peaceful, hum-

bling place. Drive, fly, train, or sail to get there. Nature does not provide binge food, so a trip to the mountains or a lake could be perfect. Plan your meals in advance. Are you going to bring your food or eat in restaurants? Bring books, paper, and anything else that the "pretend" you would have. You can even introduce yourself to people along the way as this other person. If no one can go with you, go alone. Have fun, laugh!

4. When you eventually do return home, center yourself. See the "important note" on Day 2 about things to do when you return home after having been away.

5. Write a journal entry: What parts of your "make believe" character do you want to keep for your own?

Good night: Wherever you go, you can carry your old garbage with you or leave it behind—your choice!

D A Y   1 0

Assert yourself!

Yesterday, we asked you to try being someone else. Now it's time to enjoy being who you are.

First Things First: Read the Thought for the Day, do the Morning Warmup, read the entire day's plan in this book, and work in your notebook.

Thought for the Day: I can assert myself!

Expose your feelings, opinions, and real self. It's okay if people don't always agree with you. It's okay if you don't always agree with them. It is important to say "no" sometimes. This may mean choosing different friends or living situations. Be yourself!

The Morning Warmup: Have a good, long (15–30 minutes) stretch and/or exercise workout.

Today's Options:

1. Express a strong opinion. For example, write a television network to complain about offensive programming.
2. Say "NO!" out loud to bulimia.
3. Aggressively hammer nails, chop wood, or beat up a pillow.
4. Make a new, revised list of your own.

Homework: Day 10

1. List 10–15 character traits that you like about yourself.
2. Contact a support person from Days 6 or 8 to give them an update; and, to let them be a part of your recovery.
3. Talk to a family member about your recovery from bulimia.
4. (optional) Work on your study project. This has been something we have not said much about, other than to do it. If you have gotten into this project, it is already giving you great rewards.

Good night: Ten days is a long time to follow a regime such as ours. Congratulate yourself on getting this far. Today, you released a lot of tension in many ways. Give yourself a few minutes of stretching or relaxation before going to sleep.

D A Y 1 1

I can get what I want!

When you stop being bulimic, you're not changing into someone else. You're recognizing that you are already fine, you just may not have known that. It's a subtle shift in perspective.

First Things First: Read the Thought for the Day, do the Morning Warmup, read the entire day's plan in this book, and write in your journal.

Thought for the Day: I can get what I want.

We already know that you do not want to be bulimic anymore; but what do you want? There are "wants" of a physical nature: I want a new car, I want to go on vacation, or I want to look attractive. There are also "wants" of an inner-nature: I want to be happy, I want to love myself, or I want to feel attractive. Think about your wants.

The Morning Warmup: Go for a gentle jog of about 15 minutes. Be sure to stretch first. Do not run a race!

Today's Options:

1. Buy yourself something.
2. Go somewhere you've been wanting to go.
3. Take a shower.
4. Review the options from Days 1 and 2.

Homework: Day 11

1. List fifty "I wants" including things you want to own, do, and feel. Pick five and make plans to achieve them.

2. Treat yourself to one candy bar or favorite "forbidden" food, and eat it in a special place. Any food is okay in moderation. You have to practice permitting yourself to eat without overdoing it.

3. Have a meal with a support person.

4. Make an appointment with a therapist, if you have not already done so.

5. Work at least one hour on your study project.

Good night: You've started to focus on some of your "wants." These are much healthier thoughts than obsessing about bingeing. Believe in yourself. Repeat today's Thought for the Day, and add this one: "I am overcoming bulimia!"

D A Y 1 2

Examining Values

Who you are is more important than how you look. Do you make judgments based on appearance alone? Should you? Today, let's find out.

First Things First: Read the Thought for the Day, do the Morning Warmup, read the entire day's plan in this book, and work in your notebook.

Thought for the Day: The goodness in my soul knows no size or weight.

When you choose not to be bulimic, you also choose to change your values. Probably you have been prejudiced against the way you look or how much you weigh. We have been encouraging you to love and trust your inner-self; now, is the time to accept your outer self. You can be sexual and loved with any body!

The Morning Warmup: Study your naked self in a mirror. While you are observing, realize that no one has an "ideal" body; and think of a lover who desires you exactly as you see your reflection. Even if you are not particularly artistic, draw a self-portrait of yourself.

Today's Options:

1. Exercise.

2. Go to a quiet place, such as a museum, church, or art gallery.

3. Call someone from your support list, maybe someone new.

4. Try one that has worked before!

Homework: Day 12

1. List some "happy couples" you know. Are they in love? Do you think they have a good sexual relationship? Do they have "ideal" bodies?

2. Go to a shopping mall and observe people. What do they look like? Does anyone have an "ideal" body? Do smaller people seem happier than larger people? Are there people eating-on-the-run, are they happy? Does anyone judge your appearance? Record some observations and thoughts.

3. Make a list of 5–10 myths and 5–10 rules that you want to change. A myth may be something like, "Skinny people are happier." A rule may be something like, "I can't eat ice cream at night, because I'll gain weight."

4. (optional) Buy a book with a feminist topic. Consult our Reading List for some ideas.

Good night: You can think about the past, but RIGHT NOW is what is real. This moment is what you're experiencing. Let go of the past. Old concepts don't work anymore. You can dream of a better future, but it will only come true if you strive towards that dream today.

D A Y 1 3

Clean-up Time!

You have made a strong commitment to ending your bulimia, especially if you are still following this program. When it ends tomorrow, you must continue in the same direction. Put a lot into the course these last two days, and use what you have learned to pave the way for your future.

First Things First: Read the Thought for the Day, do the Morning Warmup, read the entire day's plan in this book, and make a short journal entry.

Thought for the Day: I can make small changes with big results!

You have to change some things about your environment in order to support the changes in yourself. Notice details.

The Morning Warmup: Do a music appreciation activity. Some ideas: listen with headphones to your favorite song, play an instrument, sing, or dance.

Short Journal Entry: Write a summary of what you've learned in your study project, and reflect on your feelings about it, such as: accomplishment, intellectual fulfillment, interest, etc.

Today's Options:

1. Call a support person.
2. Work on today's homework.
3. Return to your own list.

Homework: Day 13

1. List 10–20 things which permit your bulimia, and imagine changes. These aspects of your environment may include the usual times or places you binge, friends who are negative influences, rituals, etc. (For example: If you binge while driving to work, take a bus or car pool.)

2. If there is someone from your original support list whom you've resisted telling about your recovery from bulimia, talk to them today. You are strong enough, especially if it will help your recovery.

3. Work on unfinished homework.

4. (optional) Work on your study project.

Good night: Not everyone who reads this book will do or even attempt to do this program. Many people may be attracted to the title, "A Two-Week Program to Stop Bingeing," but will shy away from actually "doing" anything. If you have followed this course for almost two weeks, you have accomplished a great feat. Think back to some of the fun moments, happy thoughts, and special places. Pleasant dreams.

D A Y   1 4

Graduation Day!

Today is Graduation Day, and you should be quite proud of yourself. Hum "Pomp and Circumstance" to yourself all day. As with most education, graduating means new challenges, independence, and some uncertainty. By doing this program, you have progressed far in your recovery from bulimia, and now we ask you to reach ever further. Bulimia will get more and more distant from your thoughts and consciousness as long as you keep making an effort.

First Things First: Read the Thought for the Day, do the Morning Warmup, and read the entire day's plan in this book.

Thought for the Day: I have accomplished something big!

If you have followed this two-week program, you have seen that you do have many abilities that may have been dormant while you obsessed about food. By being the do-er, the creator, you take power and stop feeling like a defenseless victim.

Let's summarize some of the things that you have done in this course. You've: set goals, taken initiative, examined feelings about your family, laughed, learned something new, been honest and open to others, relaxed, looked at your own values, felt sexual, identified wants, made affirmations, practiced eating without bingeing, and expressed love.

Have pride inside, your horizons are limitless.

The Morning Warmup: Read through the past thirteen Morning Warmups, and remember your experiences doing them. Do these kinds of activities every morning. Today, do any that you particularly liked.

Today's Options:

1. Do today's homework.
2. Review everyday's options, and pick one.

Homework: Day 14

1. Write about your bingeing habits of the last two weeks. What are your goals for the next few days, weeks, months, and year? Compare your remarks with those written on Day 1 about bingeing.

2. Review the course goals that you set on Day 2, and reflect on which goals were reached.

3. Carefully read through your entire notebook.

4. Outline your own program for the next week. Set goals for yourself, list options, continue accepting support, and plan some activities.

5. Final reminder: Try some form of professional therapy.

Good night: We're nostalgic writing this final message to you. Although we haven't had the opportunity to be together, we have developed a special relationship. We have shared our selves, hoping that you will be motivated in your recovery from bulimia. Think of us cheering you on while you continue making progress. With all our hearts, we wish you love, happiness, and freedom from bulimia.

We'd also like to hear from you! Nothing has given us greater satisfaction or has touched our hearts more than the beautiful letters we have received from people who have read our books during the past ten years. You can write to us care of Gürze Books (BB), P.O. Box 2238, Carlsbad CA 92008.

P A R T

III

Resources

10

Specific Advice for Loved Ones

A few words from Leigh:

Before I met Lindsey, I had done quite a few binges myself. Some of my fondest memories from childhood are of my grandmother's candy bowl and the cookie jar my mom kept filled. I won the watermelon eating contest at my high school senior class picnic, and I had a reputation among my friends for how many donuts I could eat.

When Lindsey first told me about her eating disorder, we were already in love. She said that she binge-ate, and I knew that I had found a soul-mate! Then she explained that she vomited six times daily and I understood that our binges were not the same thing.

Learning about bulimia has had a profound effect on how I feel about food. My bingeing was mindless excess, similar to a bulimic's, but I experienced enjoyment rather than guilt or anxiety and maintained a stable weight. I did not realize that other people could be so terrifed by eating. Now, I am sympathetic to all people with eating disorders, and am especially sensitive to the social and emotional pressures that they are under. I rarely binge anymore; and when I eat now, I am more acutely aware of how good it tastes, and how lucky I am to be able to enjoy it!

Many bulimics and their loved ones have asked me how I felt when Lindsey told me about her bulimia. At first, I was surprised, because I had never heard of that kind of behavior. I also underestimated how painful it was for her to be bulimic and to tell me her "horrible" secret. However, I completely loved Lindsey, and was willing to devote myself to supporting her cure. I did not want to "share" her with food, and I knew that the only way we could have a full relationship was if she stopped her bulimia. Obviously, she had to do the work, because it was her struggle, not mine. There were some trying times and emotional upheaval, but those days ended long ago. Today, she is loving, intelligent, creative, powerful, compassionate, beautiful, and sensual—I'm prejudiced!

I encourage bulimics to make their loved ones aware of their needs. Take a chance on someone close to you, they really can help! One question that we are often asked is, "What can family and friends do to help?" So, we put that question on our survey, and the responses provide some excellent guidelines:

The best way for loved ones to help me is just love me, and be there when I need them.

Be honest and supportive of the person finding a cure, though not supporting the behavior.

Look at how you feel about food, or if you contribute to your friend's or loved-one's bulimia.

I'm firmly convinced that loved ones first need to ad-

mit that this is a serious problem, and that it takes a great deal of sometimes unpleasant work for the bulimic to get better.

COMMUNICATION is very important! The person who is bulimic needs to be able to freely discuss any feelings and concerns that she might have, without feeling threatened.

Loved ones can encourage, love, support, and AC-TIVELY listen.

I think one of the most important fundamental things is to listen. I found that some people listen for about sixty seconds, and then interject their opinions and prejudices instead of openly listening and really hearing what is said.

Be up front! Tell your "sufferer" she can make a choice to stay home and abuse herself, or come along and play. Do not plan activities around food, but eat if you're hungry. Listen, share, participate, but keep it clear who has the bulimia, and whose responsibility it is to quit.

Loved ones can help by making meals pleasant rather than times for confrontations. They can protect the bulimic from being exposed to great quantities of food and rich desserts. They can de-emphasize food, and support the concept that a woman is beautiful even if she weighs more than a model. Models are not the standard of beauty.

BE THERE FOR ME! Isolation and loneliness just worsen the problem. Help me to build self-esteem and *self worth. Notice the good things and comment on them instead of harping on the bad.*

Loved ones need to help bulimics assert themselves. I needed reassurance that it was okay to say "no" to people.

Recognize that the bulimic's perfectionism and conscientiousness hides a deep sense of inferiority and self-doubt. Draw her out of her "authoritarian cocoon." Speak your mind!

Try to learn about the disorder, especially the underlying issues and causes.

Encourage the bulimic to go into therapy.

Be patient and do not expect "instant" results.

Offer to pay for therapy!

My loved ones can best help me by showing their love for me both in words and actions. I especially need to know they love me inspite of my bingeing and purging. Please don't lecture me or tell me I'm sick. I know loving me isn't easy, but please try! I need your love! I need to be accepted and smiled at.

Never make a big deal about food. Food is not the main issue; and, the sooner the family realizes this, the sooner they can help a bulimic realize it as truth.

11

National Eating Disorders Organizations

There are many national and local organizations devoted to helping people who have eating disorders. They typically offer written materials, bibliographies, newsletters, and often have referral services or sponsor support groups. We have had contact with more than twenty of these, and most of them seem to be credible and helpful. Here we list some of the largest, nonprofit organizations. These are all national, but many have local chapters:

(AABA) American Anorexia/Bulimia Association
133 Cedar Lane
Teaneck, NJ 07666
(201) 836-1800

ABC—Anorexia, Bulimia, Care, Inc.
Box 213
Lincoln Center, MA 01773
(617) 259-9767

ANAD—National Association of Anorexia Nervosa
and Associated Eating Disorders
P.O. Box 7
Highland Park, IL 60035
(312) 831-3438

ANRED—Anorexia Nervosa and Related Eating
Disorders
P.O. Box 5102
Eugene, OR 97405
(503) 344-1144

BASH—Bulimia Anorexia Self-Help, Inc.
6125 Clayton Avenue, Suite 215
St. Louis, MO 63139
(800) 227-4785 or (800) 762-3334

Center for the Study of Anorexia and Bulimia
1 West 91st Street
New York, NY 10024
(212) 595-3449

NAAS—National Anorexic Aid Society
5796 Karl Road
Columbus, OH 43229
(614) 436-1112

OA—Overeaters Anonymous Headquarters
World Services Office
2190 West 190th St.
Torrance, CA 90504
(213) 320-7941

C H A P T E R

12

A Guide for Support Groups

The format that we present here takes a group from conception through six meetings. After that, there are several options for its future. These guidelines have been adopted for use by many professional therapists and self-led bulimia groups. Even if you do not participate in a support group, these agendas contain topics and exercises which may be useful to you.

Forming the Group

There are ongoing support groups throughout the United States and Canada, and they may be found by contacting local treatment facilities, hospitals, or college health or counseling centers. Also, "Overeaters Anonymous" serves this function for many people. Additionally, the eating disorder organizations listed in the back of this book may be able to help you find a group.

As a last resort, you can use the guidelines in this section to start your own group. That means taking the initiative to gather members. A single classified advertisement in a college or local newspaper might get enough responses to fill a group. Here's how you might word the ad:

Stop your binge/vomiting. Join a free bulimia support group. Forming now to start (the date). Confidential! Call me, (Your name and phone number).

An advertisement such as this costs less than a binge, and the group might even decide to share the expense. If you run the ad a few times, there should be plenty of people interested (5–10 is a good size). Another good way to advertise for members is to place leaflets on bulletin boards in office buildings or on college campuses. Neatly present the same basic information as above on a sheet which may be photocopied. You may want to include your phone number on tear-off tabs at the bottom of the sheet.

Arrange for the first meeting, and after that, your responsibilities as leader are over.

Rules of the Group

We have devised a basic framework for the support groups, which is intended to maintain a balance of order and progression with continual positive reinforcement for participating. Professionally led groups can dispense with most of these structural technicalities, but these groups can still use the basic ideas and activities that follow in the six agendas.

At the first meeting, review the following rules:

1. Any of these rules may be changed by consensus of the group. Consensus means that everyone agrees or agrees not to stop the mutual decision of the others.
2. The underlying issue for most bulimics is not food; therefore, the following subjects should not mo-

nopolize the discussions: diets, food, bingeing, weight control, etc.

3. Each group will follow the same basic format: introduction and goals, discussion, exercises, and summary. The topics and exercises will be provided here.

4. At each meeting, different people must be appointed to the following jobs:

* facilitator (group leader to introduce each topic and call on people to speak),

*time-keeper (to keep on schedule), and

*gripe-control monitor (to interrupt anyone who is monopolizing the focus with complaints or depressing stories).

5. At the beginning of each meeting, the agenda will be reviewed and anyone who wants to add an item can do so.

6. One requirement of all group members is complete honesty.

7. No meeting shall end on a pessimistic or depressed note. If these conditions exist at the scheduled close, then a discussion or activity must be enacted to uplift the spirit of the group.

First Meeting Agenda

1. Review the rules of the group.

2. Appoint facilitator, time-keeper, and gripe-control monitor. These positions might not be necessary in professionally led groups.

3. The facilitator reviews this agenda with the group, and agenda items are added. Approximate times are allocated for each item.

4. **Introduction:** Everyone in the group introduces themselves and explains why they have joined the group. What are the reasons for attending? What are the goals of the group? Keep these introductions to a couple of minutes each.

5. **Discussion:** This meeting's topic is about the nature of support. To begin the discussion, each member of the group takes turns answering the following questions: Who has been supportive of your recovery, and what have they done that has been helpful? If anyone else knows about your bulimia, how did they react when they found out, and how did that make you feel? What are a few do's and don'ts you would recommend to someone in order to help you recover from bulimia? What will you offer to other members of the group to support them?

After the circle is complete, the group can have an open discussion about some of the things that came out in the exercise. This is not to psychoanalyze each other, but to gain insight through each other's disclosures. (20–40 minutes).

6. **Exercise:** RELAXATION! (15–20 minutes)

Everyone gets into a comfortable position, either sitting or lying down. One person talks the others through the exercise in a quiet, monotone voice, while the others relax with their eyes closed. Here is the exercise:

Take three deep breaths, inhaling, holding the breath, and exhaling to the count of ten (ten inhaling, ten holding, ten exhaling). Afterwards, breathe normally. As you inhale, feel as though you are being filled with light; and as you exhale, empty yourself of stress. Feel your body relax. Concentrate on your toes, relax them. Continue this, relaxing your feet, ankles, calves, knees, etc., until every part of the body is mentioned. Feel yourself filled with light and health, goodness, purity, contentment, power, etc. Remain in this state for several minutes before slowly reviving.

7. **Summary:** The group needs to set a time and place for the next meeting. Because this is a support group, a commitment needs to be made by the members to come to at least the first four meetings. There are guidelines here for six meetings and recommendations for continuing. Exchange phone numbers so that individuals can use each other for support outside of the group.

A Few Words About Your Progress: This first meeting may have been difficult for you. Opening up with your feelings may not have been easy or even possible. Give yourself some time; it will get easier. Individual or group therapy, medical examinations, and other steps towards self-help that are suggested in this book need to be made in addition to the support group. In any case, stick to your commitment to getting better and remember that you make your own choices.

Second Meeting Agenda

1. If appropriate, appoint a new facilitator, timekeeper, and gripe-control monitor.

2. Review the guidelines of the group and this week's agenda, and set approximate time limits for each item.

3. **Introduction:** "I wish . . . ," "I want . . . ," and "I am . . ."

Everyone takes a few minutes to complete in writing the above sentences. Then, they take turns giving their answers for "I wish . . ." one time until everyone has had a chance to answer. The circle is repeated until everyone has answered "I wish . . ." two or three times. The same is done for "I want . . ." and "I am . . ." (For the "I am . . ." portion, it is important to be positive; for example, instead of "I am a binger," say, "I am curing myself of binge eating.")

4. **Discussion:** This meeting's topic is "Family Relations." Each group member takes a few minutes to describe their family. It may be helpful to address areas such as parents' character, seeking attention, growing apart from parents, being perfect, and family meals. After everyone has had a chance to speak, open the floor to discussion and qustions. Listen carefully! Try to understand some of the reasons for your eating behavior.

5. **Exercise:** ASSERTIVENESS TO MOM OR DAD!

For the first part of this exercise, everyone writes some things that they dislike about one parent (living or dead, past or present). Then, take turns sharing answers, and continue until everyone has spoken two or three times. This exercise is then done again—this time stressing the parents' likable traits. This is continued until everyone has spoken at least three times. (Example: "I dislike how financially dependent my mother acts," and "I like that my mom cares about me.")

The second part of this exercise is a gripe session with mother or father. Get in pairs or triads and take turns spending about ten minutes in role-playing that allows you to assert yourself to your parent(s). You may bring up old wounds that have never healed, you may scream, or you may try to explain your feelings. Express your true self in a way that you have always wished you could when speaking to your actual parents. Even though this is only a role-play, try to be serious and avoid hiding your feelings. When playing the parent role, try to put yourself fully into that peron's character.

6. **Relaxation:** Take five minutes for group relaxation, led by a volunteer.

7. Set a time and place for the next meeting.

8. Share a few words about commitment to the group and the importance of being committed to at least the first four meetings. Remember that curing an eating disorder takes time and requires a commitment. Bulimia is an obsession that is best overcome with a systematic, determined approach. Group members must be able to rely on each other inside and outside of the meetings.

Do not procrastinate working on your individual steps towards getting better. If you need to seek professional therapy, have a medical examination, tell more people about your bulimia, or whatever—DO IT!

Third Meeting Agenda

1. If appropriate, appoint a new facilitator, time-keeper, and gripe-control monitor.

2. Review the guidelines of the group and this week's agenda, and set approximate time limits for each item.

3. **Introduction:** Each person spends a few minutes sharing a success story about how they stopped themselves from bingeing. If you don't have a success story, say so, and suggest something you might try to do instead of bingeing in the future. It's important to be honest!

4. **Discussion:** This meeting's topics are "ritual" and

"secrecy." Most bulimics are secretive about their food obsessions and engage in private rituals involving scales, mirrors, clothing, or food. They may even compulsively lie and steal. Each person reveals some of their secrets and answers questions.

5. **Exercise:** Repeat the progressive relaxation technique from the first meeting. The narrator talks the group into relaxation, and at that point, suggests that they see themselves in front of a mirror, and imagine themselves as a different race, a child, an old person, very ugly, the opposite sex, very beautiful, fat, thin, perfect, and finally, as light without form. Step through the mirror and feel absorbed by that light, filled with health, purity, love, contentment. Remain in this state for a few minutes before slowly reviving.

6. **Summary:** Discuss the effectiveness of the group. How can it be improved? What are everyone's feelings about the group? Are people willing to commit to attend through all six guided meetings? Does the group then want to: continue, disband, enlist a therapist (if there is not one already), etc. Start making plans now.

7. Set a time and place for the next meeting.

Fourth Meeting Agenda

1. If appropriate, appoint a new facilitator, time-keeper, and gripe-control monitor.

2. Review the guidelines of the group and this week's agenda, and set approximate time limits for each item.

3. **Introduction:** Each person shares a brief story about something they have done or experienced since the support group began, which was a positive step towards their recovery. This may be an action, thought, or feeling.

4. **Discussion:** "The Media, Feminism, and Food."

This is an open-ended discussion. Consider these questions: Why are bulimics mainly women? How does the media affect your body image? Is the media's treatment of women an honest reflection of our culture's values? Try to keep comments related to personal experiences.

5. **Exercise:** Every person takes turns changing an ad that is demeaning towards women into a non-sexist presentation. Allow a few minutes for everyone to jot down their ideas. For example, the diet soft drink ad that shows thin women taking their clothes off would be more honest if men and women of all colors and sizes were portrayed in the ad too.

6. **Discuss the future of the group.** Initially, everyone was asked to make at least a four-meeting commitment to the group, and this is the fourth meeting. There are still two more meeting agendas provided here. What are everyone's feelings about the group? Are people willing to attend those additional guided meetings? What direction is the group going to take. Is the group open to new members? A decision should be reached by the next meeting. Set a time and place for the next meeting.

7. **Summary:** What can we do as individuals on a daily basis to improve our self-image?

Fifth Meeting Agenda

1. If appropriate, appoint a new facilitator, time-keeper, and gripe-control monitor.

2. Review the guidelines of the group and this week's agenda, and set approximate time limits for each item.

3. **Introduction:** Each person shares positive experiences with self-help ideas or professional therapy.

4. **Discussion:** "Feelings are not good or bad, they just are."

Bulimics are often "people pleasers" who tend to keep their real feelings hidden. They are said to "swallow their feelings" instead of being honest about them. To get this discussion started, go around the group and allow everyone to name a kind of feeling (happiness, fear, excitement, etc.). Give everyone the chance to name a few. Then, discuss these topics and others that develop. How can we identify feelings as they happen rather than hiding from them? There are specific ways of coping with difficult feelings. What are some suggestions?

5. **Exercise:** Fill in this sentence and repeat the exercise several times: "When I want to do something for myself, I . . ."

6. **Summary:** Resolve the group's future. This is a good time to consider inviting a trained therapist to the next meeting, if that has not already been done.

7. Set a time and place for the next meeting.

8. Share you feelings about the group's effectiveness.

Sixth Meeting Agenda

1. Appoint a new facilitator, time-keeper, and gripe-control monitor.

2. Review the guidelines of the group and this week's agenda, and set approximate time limits for each item.

3. **Introduction:** In what positive ways have you changed since joining the group? New members should

answer the introduction questions from the first meeting's agenda. Everyone takes a turn answering.

4. **The Future of the Group:** If your group's future is uncertain at this time, determining its future is a top priority. Spend as much time as needed to finish up this matter. If you do not get to the discussion topic, that is all right.

5. **Discussion:** "Becoming Independent."

Women in our society often feel dependent, emotionally, economically, and in other ways (on parents, husbands, employers, etc.). Are the members of the group moving towards independence? How? This is an open-ended discussion.

6. **Exercise:** Repeat the relaxation exercise from the third meeting.

C H A P T E R
13

Reading List

Bauer, Barbara; Anderson, Wayne; and Hyatt, Robert. *Bulimia Book for Therapist and Client,* Muncie, IN: Accelerated Development, 1986.

Beattie, Melody. *Codependent No More.* New York: Harper/Hazelden, 1987.

Bennett, William, and Gurin, Joel. *The Dieter's Dilemma.* New York: Basic Books, 1982.

Bradshaw, John. *Bradshaw On: The Family.* Deerfield Beach, FL: Health Communications, 1988.

Bradshaw, John. *Healing the Shame.* Deerfield Beach, FL: Health Communications, 1989.

Brownell, Kelly, and Foreyt, John. *Handbook of Eating Disorders.* New York: Basic Books, 1986.

Bruckner-Gordon, Fredda; Gangi, Barbara; and Wallman, Geraldine. *Making Therapy Work.* New York: Harper & Row, 1988.

Buscaglia, Leo. *Living, Loving & Learning.* New York: Ballantine Books, 1982.

Chernin, Kim. *The Hungry Self: Women, Eating & Identity.* New York: Harper & Row, 1985.

Chernin, Kim. *The Obsession.* New York: Harper & Row, 1981.

Davis, Martha; Eshelman, Elizabeth; and McKay, Matthew. *The Relaxation & Stress Reduction Workbook (Third Edition).* Oakland, CA: New Harbinger, 1988.

Ebbitt, Joan. *The Eating Illness Workbook.* Park Ridge, IL: Parkside Publishing, 1987.

Fanning, Patrick. *Visualization for Change*. Oakland, CA: New Harbinger, 1988.

Freedman, Rita. *BodyLove*. New York: Harper & Row, 1988.

Garner, David, and Garfinkel, Paul (editors). *Handbook of Psychotherapy for Anorexia Nervosa & Bulimia*. New York: Guilford Press, 1985.

Garner, David, and Garfinkel, Paul (editors). *The Role of Drug Treatments for Eating Disorders*. New York: Brunner/Mazel Publishers, 1987.

Hall, Lindsey, and Cohn, Leigh. *Self-Esteem: Tools for Recovery*. Carlsbad, CA: Gürze Books, 1989.

Hall, Lindsey, and Cohn, Leigh (editors). *Recoveries: True Stories by People Who Conquered Addictions and Compulsions*. Carlsbad, CA: Gürze Books, 1987.

Hampshire, Elizabeth. *Freedom From Food*. Park Ridge, IL: Parkside Publishing, 1988.

Hollis, Judi. *Fat is a Family Affair*. San Francisco: Harper/Hazelden, 1985.

Johnson, Craig, and Connors, Mary. *The Etiology and Treatment of Bulimia Nervosa*. New York: Basic Books, 1987.

Kano, Susan. *Making Peace With Food*. New York: Harper & Row, 1989.

Lakoff, Robin, and Scherr, Raquel. *Face Value: The Politics of Beauty*. Boston: Routledge & Kegan Paul, 1984.

Latimer, Jane Evans. *Living Binge-Free*. Boulder, CO: LivingQuest, 1988.

Lerner, Harriet Goldhor. *The Dance of Anger*. New York: Harper & Row, 1985.

Messinger, Lisa. *Biting the Hand That Feeds Me*. Novato, CA: Arena Press, 1986.

McKay, Matthew, and Fanning, Patrick. *Self-Esteem*. Oakland, CA: New Harbinger, 1987.

Muktananda, Swami. *Where Are You Going?* South Fallsburg, NY: 1981.

Nakken, Craig. *The Addictive Personality*. San Francisco: Harper/Hazelden, 1988.

Orbach, Susie. *Fat is a Feminist Issue*. New York: Padington Press, 1978.

Peck, M. Scott. *The Road Less Traveled*. New York: Touchstone, 1978.

Pope, Harrison, and Hudson, James. *New Hope for Binge Eaters*. New York: Harper & Row, 1984.

Root, Maria; Fallon, Patricia; and Friedrich, William. *Bulimia: A Systems Approach to Treatment*. New York: Basic Books, 1986.

Roth, Geneen. *Breaking Free from Compulsive Eating*. New York: Bobbs-Merrill, 1984.

Roth, Geneen. *Feeding the Hungry Heart*. New York: Bobbs-Merrill, 1984.

Sacker, Ira, and Zimmer, Marc. *Dying to be Thin*. New York: Warner Books, 1987.

Sandbeck, Terence. *The Deadly Diet*. Oakland, CA: New Harbinger, 1986.

Sanford, Linda Tschirhart, and Donovan, Mary Ellen. *Women & Self-Esteem*. New York: Viking Penguin, 1984.

Seid, Roberta Pollack. *Never Too Thin*. New York: Prentice Hall, 1989.

Siegel, Michele; Brisman, Judith; and Weinshel, Margot. *Surviving an Eating Disorder*. New York: Harper and Row, 1988.

Thoele, Sue Patton. *The Courage to be Yourself*. Nevada City, CA: Pyramid Press, 1988.

Valette, Brett. *A Parent's Guide to Eating Disorders*. New York: Walker Publishing, 1988.

Weiss, Lillie; Katzman, Melanie; and Wolchik, Sharlene. *You Can't Have Your Cake and Eat it Too*. Saratoga, CA: R & E Publishers, 1986.

White, Marlene Boskind, and White, William. *Bulimarexia: The Binge-Purge Cycle*. New York: W. W. Norton, 1983.

Whitfield, Charles. *Healing the Child Within*. Deerfield, FL: Health Communications, 1987.

Woodman, Marion. *Addiction to Perfection*. Toronto, Canada: Inner City Books, 1982.

**Many of these books and others, as well, are directly available from "The Eating Disorders Bookshelf Catalogue," which we edit and distribute. It is regularly updated to include new titles. You may send for a *free copy* by writing to:

Eating Disorders Bookshelf Catalogue (BB)
P.O. Box 2238
Carlsbad, CA 92008

Index

Alcoholism, 15
Anorexia nervosa:
  clinical diagnosis, 13–14
Bulimia:
  antidepressants, treatment, 21
  binges, typical, 14–15, 34, 37, 42, 44
  causes, 5–6, 7–13, 70
    biological, genetic: see heredity
  criteria for clinical diagnosis, 3–4
  cultural background, 6–13, 31–33, 123
  emotional pressures, 86
  emotional side-effects, 6
  families of bulimics, 6, 31–32, 51, 69–73, 126
  history, 3

  incidence of, 5–6
  incidence of in males, 4, 10
  length of, 19, 20
  a personal history, 30–54
  personality traits, 6–7, 9
  physical "high," 15–16
  physical side-effects, 4–5, 43, 59–63, 81
  purges, types of, 4, 44
  recovery, 48–54
  rituals, 17
  secretive nature, 17, 40–41, 68–69
  Self-image, 36–37, 50–51, 52, 53, 82–83
  symptoms, 3–4
  weight change, 23–26
Dehydration, 4, 5
Diagnostic and Statistical Manual of Mental Disorders (DSM-III), 3

About the Authors

Lindsey Hall, a graduate of Stanford University, is a recovered bulimic who lectures extensively on eating disorders across the country. She has appeared on national television and radio shows. Her husband, Leigh Cohn, is a graduate of Northwestern University and the publisher of Gürze Books.

They have co-authored a number of books, including *Dear Kids of Alcoholics, Recoveries,* and *Self-Esteem Tools for Recovery.* They have two sons and reside in Carlsbad, CA.

BANTAM BOOKS
ON ADDICTION AND RECOVERY

ADDICTION

The most up-to-date information from the leading experts in the field.

800-COCAINE
Mark S. Gold, M.D.
From the leading expert on cocaine abuse and treatment, an informative, prescriptive manual with hard facts on America's fastest-growing drug problem.
34388-2 • *Large Format Paperback* • $3.50/$3.95 in Canada

THE FACTS ABOUT DRUGS AND ALCOHOL
Mark S. Gold, M.D.
The bestselling author of 800-COCAINE provides concise, medically proven information on marijuana, heroin, LSD, crack, and other commonly abused substances.
27826-6 • *Paperback* • $3.95/$4.95 in Canada

UNDER THE INFLUENCE
A Guide to the Myths and Realities of Alcoholism
James R. Milam, Ph.D., and Katherine Ketcham
This groundbreaking classic emphasizes treating alcoholism as a physiological disease and offers information on how to tell if someone is an alcoholic, treatment, and recovery.
27487-2 • *Paperback* • $4.95/$5.95 in Canada

SEX, DRUGS & AIDS
Oralee Wachter
For every family—offers advice and dispels dangerous myths about AIDS, by the author of *No More Secrets for Me.*
34454-4 • *Large Format Paperback* • $3.95/$4.95 in Canada

RECOVERY

From alcoholism to eating disorders, books that offer concrete tools for physical, emotional, and spiritual recovery.

LIVING ON THE EDGE
A Guide to Intervention for Families with Drug and Alcohol Problems
Katherine Ketcham and Ginny Lyford Gustafson
From two renowned professionals, compassionate, step-by-step advice on every facet of family intervention, from preparation to finding the right treatment options and support groups.
34606-7 • *Large Format Paperback* • $7.95/$9.95 in Canada

EATING WITHOUT FEAR
A Guide to Understanding and Overcoming Bulimia
Leigh Cohn and Lindsey Hall
Warm and supportive, this book helps the reader set realistic goals and discusses support systems as well as how to establish healthier eating habits. Includes a two-week "Stop bingeing" program and advice for family and friends.
28377-4 • *Paperback* • $3.95/$4.95 in Canada

RECOVERING
How to Get and Stay Sober
L. Ann Mueller, M.D., and Katherine Ketcham
An essential resource for alcoholics and those who love them, a comprehensive and compassionate guide to new treatment programs that have helped many alcoholics achieve lasting sobriety.
34303-3 • *Large Format Paperback* • $8.95/$11.95 in Canada

RECLAIMING OUR LIVES
Hope for Adult Survivors of Incest
Carol Poston and Karen Lison
A comprehensive, inspiring, and supportive guide with a concrete, 14-step program for healing by an incest survivor and a therapist.
28497-5 • *Paperback* • $4.95/$5.95 in Canada

THE TWELVE STEPS REVISITED
Ronald L. Rogers, Chandler Scott McMillin, Morris A. Hill
An inspiring new interpretation of the 12 steps of Alcoholics Anonymous that clearly illustrates the path toward recovery that has worked for so many millions of people.
34733-0 • *Large Format Paperback* • $6.95/$8.95 in Canada

DON'T HELP
A Positive Guide to Working with the Alcoholic
Ronald L. Rogers and Chandler Scott McMillin
For counselors, health-care professionals, and families, a definitive and practical guide to working with the alcoholic.
34716-0 • *Large Format Paperback* • $8.95/$11.95 in Canada

ADULT CHILDREN

Essential reading for the millions who grew up in dysfunctional families.

THE ADULT CHILDREN OF ALCOHOLICS SYNDROME
Wayne Kritsberg
Real help and hope for adult children in a complete self-help program that shows how to recognize and remedy the effects of the dysfunctional family.
27279-9 • *Paperback* • $3.95/$4.95 in Canada

BECOMING YOUR OWN PARENT
The Solution for Adult Children of Alcoholic and Other Dysfunctional Families
Dennis Wholey
Television host Dennis Wholey, author of THE COURAGE TO CHANGE and himself an "adult child," takes us inside a series of meetings where fourteen men and women learn to find within themselves the validation and nurturance they were denied as children. Also offers the wisdom of a dozen nationally recognized experts on recovery.
34788-8 • *Large Format Paperback* • $8.95/$11.95 in Canada

HEALING FOR ADULT CHILDREN OF ALCOHOLICS
Sara Hines Martin
A groundbreaking work that examines the spiritual and emotional healing that must take place for complete recovery from the ACOA Syndrome.
"Truly commendable."—Dr. Robert H. Schuller
28246-8 • *Paperback* • $4.50/$5.50 in Canada